UNDER GEMINI

a memoir by

ISABEL BOLTON

STEERFORTH PRESS
SOUTH ROYALTON, VERMONT

For information about permission to reproduce
selections from this book,write to:
Steerforth Press L.C., P.O. Box 70,
South Royalton, Vermont 05068.

Library of Congress Cataloging-in-Publication Data
Bolton, Isabel, 1883–1975.
Under Gemini / Isabel Bolton. — 1st pbk. ed.
p. cm.
ISBN 1-883642-68-X (alk. paper)
    1. Bolton, Isabel, 1883–1975—Childhood and youth.
2. Women authors, American—20th century—Family relation-
ships. 3. Women authors, American—20th century—Biography.
4. Sisters—Death—Pschological aspects. 5. Bolton, Isabel,
1883–1975—Family. 6. Orphans—United States—Biography.
7. Drowning victims—United States. 8. Twins—Psychology.
9. Loss (Psychology) I. Title.
        PS3525.I553Z474   1999
        815'.5209—dc21
        [B]   98-31406
                                   CIP

Manufactured in the United States of America

FIRST PAPERBACK EDITION

To My Incomparable Friend
Tobias Schneebaum

Foreword

$\mathcal{W}$HEN I EVOKE those hours of childhood to live in them once more, it is not myself I see before me — it is she, the living image of myself, and there I stand revealed in all the sharp intensity of what the moment brought of pain or joy or curiosity or wonder or decision. I see my own face, my own dark eyes and hair, I hear my voice, my intonations and tricks of speech. The words that issue from her tongue are mine. Her expressions mantle, as I remember it, my countenance. Attuned to the same vibrations, with nerves that responded to the same dissonances and harmonies, we were one in body and in soul. What happened to one of us happened at the same instant to the other and both of us recognized exactly how each experience had registered in the other's heart and mind.

It was never I but always we. It was never you or I but both of us. Never mine or yours but always ours. We were seldom referred to by those we lived among as Mary or as Grace but as the twins — I was Mary, she was Grace. This may be so.

There is a legend that once the ribbons we wore upon our wrists to establish our identity were misplaced while we were being bathed. Our nurse, Mathilda, unable to tell which twin was which, called upon our mother to decide. She replaced the ribbons, saying I was Mary and the other child was Grace. Let us assume that she was right, for I was christened Mary and my twin was christened Grace; and so, awarding her the honor of having entered this world five minutes before I did, I will attempt to recapture the memories of our life together on this earth.

One

THERE IS A ROOM darkened against the light
and on the couch a gentleman with a dark mustache is lying
fast asleep. He snores. Behind the couch I kneel and kneeling
with me is my other self. Identical excitement, terror, fearful
joy invades us. We wait. I watch my duplicate arise and I am
rising with her. There is a moment for decision and then a
swift resolve — a dreadful sharing of the consequences that
will follow the awful act we contemplate; and then, excitement
urging us, we spit directly in our father's upturned face. He
rises. We flee while panic overtakes us and then a sudden darkness, the waters of continuing experience engulf our father
and his wrath. We have no further memory of him whatever.

A second memory — a brightly lighted room, a large
double bed, a dressing table covered with glittering objects —
and here we are together and with us is a presence. She moves

about and there is for us a radiant glamour in all that she is doing — our mother dressing to go out. Arrayed in all her splendor and carrying in her hand a nail file, she crosses the room and flicks the nail file several times upon the counterpane. We are entranced. We watch her spellbound, but in an instant she is gone and like our father is covered by the waters of continuing experience.

Now from the darkness of unremembered days another memory emerges. It is summer. There is space around us. Blue sky and sea and air; there is a foghorn blowing, there is a donkey and a donkey cart and Mathilda. The hooves of the little donkey make a delightful sound upon the road. The donkey goes hee-haw, hee-haw, and the sound of his braying is inextricably mingled with the sound of the foghorn; these sounds are joyously telling us that we are at the seaside and in this donkey cart with pails and shovels on our way to the beach.

Out of summer and the halcyon days again a memory — an event sharp and irrevocable. The donkey is on his way to carry us together with Mathilda to stay with Mrs. Emory. The donkey brays. We laugh and Mathilda chides us for our laughing. We are excited but our excitement is invaded by a curious sense of sadness induced by Mathilda's mood and her sorrowful German reprimands. Suddenly the drive has ended and we are sitting on the floor in a sunny upper room playing with our dolls when Mrs. Emory enters. She is weeping. She tells us that our mother and our father are dead, that they were very ill and now have gone to live with God. Her voice, tuned to accord with this melancholy information, vibrates mournfully within us and though we are incapable of understanding exactly what she says we start to cry. I look at Grace and know that I am crying too. The tears stream down our faces. We wail. Mrs. Emory, attempting to be cheerful, begins to talk about the joys of heaven and how our parents are waiting there for us, there among the angels and the clouds. We must not cry, she reiterates. And thereupon we cease our wailing and resume our playing with the dolls upon the floor.

Memories and time which it would seem propels them are unaccountable. They advance and retreat, but now their tides have carried us along so far as to give us an awareness of who and where we are. Not, as you might expect, two children, but one, who takes with her wherever she may be another person's sensibilities. She knows herself to be that other person; whatever may be occurring to her she receives in double measure; this complete awareness of her other self is a familiar state of being; without it each twin would lose her own identity, which consists in short of being one and indivisible.

We find ourselves in our grandmother's home. Here there are terraces and lawns, trees, shadows and sunlight. There is a yellow house; rooms appear to be well furnished; beds and tables, sofas and sideboards, chairs and pictures on the wall are in accustomed places.

People emerge — voices, faces; we give them names, endow them with personalities and become aware of their relationship to us. And so we take them, as children will, into our consciousness, absorb them, grow acquainted with them, but always with the acutest realization that the knowing process is a joint enterprise that is the business of loving and hating, of being profoundly compromised with other individuals surrounding us.

Our grandmother is old. She is small and very fragile. She wears a black dress buttoned to the throat, a white ruching at her neck, a snow-white cap upon her head. She sits by an open fire wrapped in a soft white shawl. She is always kind and gentle. There is something about her presence, a sort of sadness for which we seem in a manner responsible. Being with her prompts us to good behavior. She is accompanied by a stout old lady with a red face and white hair (touched with a peculiar tinge of saffron) that is parted and well plastered to her head. Our grandmother calls her Julia and we are told to say Aunt Julia whenever we address her. Her principal function seems to be to protect our grandmother from the children to whom she has offered her home. There are five of us who are glumly referred to by Aunt Julia as the Miller children.

Philip is the oldest. He is terrible; nobody can make him mind. He sits for long periods at a time reading in the library. His eyes are on his book but he watches everyone around him; he likes to see how people act. He enjoys torturing others, especially Grace and me. His favorite method of doing this is to pronounce a single word. We always know when he is about to do this and he loves to draw the torture out. Slowly, very slowly, his face grows rigid, he begins to clench his hands, he opens his mouth — "CHOLERA," he says in a sepulchral whisper, making at us with his clutching hands as though about to grip us with this fearful malady. Nobody can possibly imagine the terror we endure. Then too he likes to torture Ellen, the rabbit who lives under the veranda. He'll thrust at her through the openings in the lattice with a long spiked pole. Round and round under the veranda runs poor Ellen, and round and round the house runs Philip, panting, thrusting with his pole.

Rebecca is the next oldest to Philip. Not being a boy and not being a twin, she walks alone. She is very emotional and weeps a great deal. It is likely she enjoys her unhappiness. She says she does not belong to our family. She plays the piano beautifully. She takes lessons twice a week with Miss Lena Warner, a daughter of our grandmother's friend. On these occasions scales and lovely tunes can be heard issuing from the south parlor. She adores her music. She says that it is all she has. She has remarkable eyes. Sometimes they are gray and sometimes blue and at other times the pupils grow larger and larger till they are the color of dark purple violets.

James, who is the youngest next to us, is perfectly charming. He is very handsome — like his grandfather, they say, like his Uncle James. He has brown eyes the color of chestnuts and a shock of brown hair of a somewhat lighter shade. He appears to be cheerful and whistles a great deal but at times he is extremely thoughtful. He says funny things without laughing at them himself. We have a great affection for our brother James.

Two

At WHAT AGE or in which year the human event emerges, it is often difficult to say, but with this wondrous apparatus of our twinship, life goes on accumulating experience and is always full of drama. It comes to us from all directions, offering us many discoveries and holding in wait for us new information.

Our curiosity is immense. There are no means we will not try to widen our understanding — thoughts, feelings, sensations, that business of the heart receiving from the nerves each new enlightenment. We are avid for conversation; indeed, it seems that everything we hear and the voices to which we listen convey astonishing initiations.

People come and go, friends of our grandmother's, old ladies quietly dressed, refined, enunciating words with great precision. There is Mrs. Morton, who has an air in spite of dingy clothes and ancient bonnets of being somebody — a personage. And Mrs. Warner, very animated, fussy, trying to maintain an air of great gentility. They call each other by their first names and it is odd to learn they are Lena and Lucy and odder still to hear them call our grandmother Rebecca. They are always discussing Jim and Anna, our guardians; they wonder what they will advise our grandmother to do about the five of us. Mrs. Warner thinks they ought to take us under their roof; there is plenty of money at their disposal and what with that enormous place at Goshen and all the extra rooms at Chestnut Street it would not be too difficult to manage. We are too great a charge upon our grandmother. Aunt Julia emphatically agrees. Our grandmother is adamant — as long as she remains alive and this house is hers to shelter us, we will stay. Mrs. Morton thinks our grandmother is right; the joy it gives her to have Grace's children growing up around her far outweighs the strain.

Our Uncle James — was he the Jim to whom the old ladies and our grandmother so frequently referred? Who had, so it appeared, visited Grandma just after our arrival at Maple Street? Did we remember his presence in this new home of ours? Had he been closeted for hours at a time with her making plans, coming to decisions? And, departing then for Europe, leaving no trace behind him except perhaps the vague impression of a little gentleman dressed in black who had upon occasions asked us silly questions?

We are uncertain when it was he came back a second time, bringing with him our Aunt Anna and the rest of his amazing family, but it was the winters and the early springs that were associated with their visits, for they disappeared during the summer months when, we gathered, they were staying at that place called Goshen, which whenever mentioned, an inkling, just an inkling, of remembrance brushed our minds. Was it there and to that farmhouse that the donkey, hee-hawing all the way and striking his sharp hooves along the road, had carried us?

It was difficult at first to take these relatives of ours as being important in their relationship to us. They had an almost apparitional quality, coming and going, disappearing as they did for months at a time and then again returning. What made their presence at once unreal and glamorous was that they came to us out of Europe, out of Paris, France, and everything about their appearance — their clothes, the attitudes they struck, their very smells, wafting about delicious perfumes and sachets and scented soaps — heightened their unreality. Their daughters, our cousins Anna and Rebecca, seemed to be endowed with fairy-tale qualities such as our imaginations were accustomed to bestow upon our paper dolls. As for their son, Chapin, we'd never seen his like before — compared to our rough-and-tumble brothers, in his beautifully cut clothes and with his French schooling he seemed altogether too grand to claim us for his cousins.

Colorful indeed were their arrivals. They came in fabulous vehicles — if there was snow upon the ground, in a sleigh resembling a swan in structure. Rounding our drive amid the music of silver bells and jingling harnesses, they would draw up to our front door. Pushing aside their fur robes Aunt Anna and Uncle James would alight from their swan boat. We would walk behind them up the veranda steps, follow them into the house and into the library, where we would watch them greet our grandmother.

In the presence of our uncle we were never without uneasiness, always uncertain as to how we should answer the questions we were never quite able to understand. For what reason did he ask us whose chicken coop we were about to rob, and what did he mean in inquiring how many beans we had just put up our nose? Though he was extremely short, his elegance was overpowering — his black suit, his black spats and gloves and a black pearl in his black cravat, his startling eyes, large and dark and brilliant, and his hair and mustache quite white but his eyebrows black as black, with such small bands and his small feet shod to perfection. He was the most remarkable miniature gentleman anyone could imagine.

The spectacle of our Aunt Anna affected us quite differently. Whatever charm and geniality she might have had was compressed, laced in, buttoned up, suppressed. Her clothes fitted her tightly; they were handsome and well brushed, not glamorous at all but with their own special elegance. She did not approve of charm; she listened rather disapprovingly to Uncle Jim and always asked practical questions, saying, "My dear Jim, I don't agree. This should not be done. I don't approve." She said, "You must" and "You must not" with emphasis.

She sometimes invited us to take a sleigh ride with her; well tucked in by those ample rugs, one on either side of her, we received the impact of her personality. It was, curiously enough, the smells accompanying these rides that brought an all-pervading sense not only of this lady's wealth but of her importance. Emanating from her, always present in the cold crisp air, was the aroma of cedarwood and camphor and something else that seemed to be Aunt Anna's very self; its oppressive effect made us, in spite of the gay jingling of bells and the silent slipping of the runners, eager to have the long ordeal beside her over.

Through our avidity for conversation, sitting silent together on a chair or a sofa, playing unnoticed on the floor, listening to intonations, sensing approval or disapproval, we learned a great deal about the history of our unremembered days.

What with the big words and our small acquaintance with them, what was there that we could gather from all this grown up conversation? We had lived in a great city, in a large house; we had had far too many servants; it had not been necessary for the boys and Rebecca to have had Annie Wilkenny, their German governess; there were many things that had not been necessary. Charlie Miller, though a brilliant man with a fine future, should not have worked so hard or died so young. He was most improvident. Indeed, he was responsible for all the problems presented to our guardians, because he was, and to his great discredit, a Miller.

Was Charlie Miller, who was so grossly extravagant and had left no provision for his children, the gentleman asleep upon the couch whose wrath we had once so terribly aroused?

There was much that we did not understand — listening, communicating, watching the faces, expressions; the heart had gathered more than the mind was able to interpret. There were moments when we felt that life was bringing a double portion of everything — too much drama, too much color, too many tableaux, an excess of information. It was more than we could bear. Suddenly our emotions erupted, exploding in a simultaneous performance, a kind of crazy circus in which without knowing who was doing what, thumbs appeared on the ends of noses, fingers waggled in the air, tongues protruded from our lips and clownish somersaults and handsprings earned for us the reputation of being the most outrageous show-offs in the world.

Three

THERE WAS ANOTHER world to which we could escape, and with what rapture we found ourselves outdoors, released from tensions too frequently endured! The blue air, the movement of winds and clouds and shadows, the song of birds produced in us a celestial climate natural to our heart.

Our grandmother's premises were spacious — the broad front lawn with its great companionable elms, the one big maple and the horse chestnut tree with the beautiful red blossoms and the hummingbirds that darted above them in the season of their blooming, the lawn behind, which reached to the edge of the terraces (the "bankings," as we called them).

There were apple and pear trees of different varieties — Astrachan and Baldwin, Bartlett and Seckel — arbors where Concord grapes and Delawares hung from their trellised vines in abundant clusters. And all these vines and fruit trees, because of lack of pruning, had grown to a certain wildness — an extravagance of inattention.

At the foot of the bankings the large garden, very neglected, had gone to seed; once it had been tended with an eye to order and the proper care of vegetables and flower beds. Now the strawberry beds were filled with weeds and scraggly plants with a scant output of berries. In the rose garden the bushes were much diminished and only a few varieties bloomed each year. The asparagus bed had grown to a jungle, with seeding plumes of slender stems and scarcely any edible stalks. The rhubarb plants, their red transparent stems supporting leaves like palm-leaf fans, shadowed the ground beneath them.

Was it May? Could we find enough asparagus for supper? Or was it June and were there strawberries to pick? No, it was too hot and there were only a few of them anyway. We might crawl into a small yellow house at the confines of our grandmother's property. Yes, we might do that.

Off we ran to the dilapidated gardener's cottage almost buried in the overgrowing lilac and syringa bushes. The syringa was in bloom. We stopped to smell the rich intoxicating fragrance. How beautiful all these blossoms with the yellow pollen luminous through their alabaster petals. Hot, drenched in summer, sticky with strawberry juice and pollen, we flopped down to rest a moment before climbing the bankings to get in on the second floor, for at the back of the house were windows with broken panes through which we could enter.

"Push me, Mary — give me a boost."

"Pull me — give me your hand, Grace."

The rooms were empty. There were several hornet nests; spiders had draped their webs across the windows and spun them in the corners, trapping flies and hornets whose carcasses hung loosely in their meshes. The paper was peeling off the walls.

What was there in this empty house, bereft of human content, that made us want to sit down together on the floor and smell it, to drain it of its mysteries?

Who had lived in it? Had Grandma had a gardener? Where was he now? Exploring these queer, these pleasurable sensations, we were lost to time, entranced by questions so closely shared.

A whiff of syringa blown in through the broken windows brought us to our feet. We climbed over the sill and were out in the fresh air again. Up the terraces we ran to the lawn above, then down another steeper bank until we came to the old stable yard, the cobbles overgrown with grass and moss. The stable door was open. There were evidences that once there had been horses and a coachman. A small stall for a pony. Our mother must have had a pony. We sniffed and pried. Some rickety stairs led to a big loft above; it was empty of hay and the coachman's room had nothing in it but an iron bed with rusty springs. What should we do next? Out we ran across the cobbles once more, up the terrace and over the lawn in the direction of the Callenders' house, whose lawn joined ours with nothing to mark the boundary but the stump of an old elm tree. Julia Callender had red hair. She was our playmate, and Arthur, familiarly called Dullah, played with our brothers. We loved to watch their games but were never allowed to join them. They were rough and terrible.

As much as we loved being outdoors, it was often a great pleasure to reenter the house; a gracious home it was indeed. The rooms were full of objects that had stories of their own, and as time went on became crowded with memories and associations.

To the right was the south parlor. Being there unaccompanied by an adult gave us a sense of tempting providence. There were so many things we must not do. We were forbidden to "sit upon the chintz," which was tantamount to saying that we could not sit down at all, as the chairs and the large three-backed sofa were covered with this expensive imported material; so many objects we must not touch — treasures brought back from Europe (which greatly heightened their importance). In front of a window on a marble pedestal was the bust of a little girl — our mother; she had gone to Italy when she was eight years old. She looked at us with her marble smile, her marble eyes, as if to tell us that she too had been in Europe as well as all the other treasures that adorned the room. Over the mantel was a copy of the famous Carlo Dolci Madonna in a large gilt frame. Near the bust of our mother was a painting by Rubens of two adorable fat cherubs writing on a scroll. They were naked and stood with their chubby legs far apart. We never looked at this beguiling picture with an entirely guiltless conscience. There were many other objects brought from Italy — a bronze Mercury, winged at cap and heel, was about to take off into space — a dying gladiator lingered for our benefit in his final agonies. Smaller objects were placed on various tables — the leaning tower of Pisa executed in ivory suggested that it might be made to lean a little farther, a black marble paperweight from Naples displayed a rose so exquisitely painted that we could scarcely resist smashing the shining casement to find out if the beautiful pink flower was actually real. Completing the list of prohibitions was the big square piano, where Rebecca played passionate preludes and sonatas.

Across the hall was the "little parlor," a very pretty room, the principal feature of which was an Aubusson carpet. At

Christmastime when the great tree stood in the center of the room, a white sheet was spread to protect it from the drippings of pine needles and many lighted candles.

Sliding doors, generally open, led to the library, which was the most lived in of all the downstairs rooms. Here we were accustomed to find our grandmother, her white shawl draped over her shoulders, sitting before the fire. Opposite was the dining room; over the mantel was our favorite painting — some ragged boys sitting on the ground surrounded by baskets full of grapes; one boy, his head thrown back, held a luscious cluster just above his open mouth.

On the next floor there were four large bedrooms. The hall was wide and at the end of it there was a large window facing the lawn between the houses and the western sky. To the left was Aunt Julia's bedroom, to the right Rebecca's. She owned it by herself. Our room was next to hers and there we slept in a large double bed. A small sewing room adjoined it, occupied at present by Mathilda. Across from our room was our grandmother's bedroom. This room was haunted by three little girls whose portraits hung on the walls, our aunts Rebecca, Sarah and Laura. Over the fireplace and facing Grandma's bed was Aunt Rebecca, gorgeously arrayed in a red velvet gown; her arms and neck were bare and she appeared to be dressed for a ball. She was, so Grandma told us, a very handsome child. Laura, also with bare arms and a low neck, was dressed in blue; she had brown curls and looked to us exactly the age of her sister Rebecca. Sarah, all in airy white, seemed neither older nor younger than her sisters. According to Mathilda, each of these ghostly children had died of summer complaint occasioned by sitting on the wet grass. How many times, we wondered, had we sat upon the wet grass? The more we thought about them, the sadder it seemed — why should *they* have died so young?

The double weight of sensibility, the impact of living moments — the smell of bread rising from the kitchen, of gingerbread just taken from the oven, the sound of squirrels scurrying on the veranda roof, shadows of leaves on the bedroom walls, flames in the open fireplaces, the all-pervading smell of burning logs, the sense of unseen presences — all combined to make us feel so safe, so sheltered in this comfortable home our grandmother had given us.

Four

*I*T'S COMING FASTER!"

"We can't see the steeple or the trees at the edge of the bankings."

"Now we can't even see the big tree nearest the house."

Not knowing whether one or the other or no one at all was talking, we stood by the window in the dining room watching the behavior of the great storm. The wind howled around the corners of the house and swirled the snow in every direction, making a cloud of darkness that hid the branches of the trees. We ran from one room to another, highly excited.

"Oh, make it keep on! Let the blizzard get bigger and bigger!" was the fervent prayer we shared in common.

In the library we found Grandmother sitting by the open fire, her white shawl drawn round her shoulders.

"It *is* a blizzard, isn't it, Grandma?"

She said she'd never known a storm in all her years more wild than this. We hugged her joyously, comforted in the midst of new and exhilarating dangers. We hoped the storm would continue forever.

In the morning we discovered that the snow was still falling and the wind howling louder than ever. No postman, no milkman, no groceries arrived. How long since we had been able to see the street and the people passing by and even trees on the front lawn? All the horsecars had stopped running on Maple Street. There was no sound of sleigh bells in the air.

Would we have enough to eat? Would there be kerosene enough to fill the lamps? When would the milkman and the groceryman arrive? Presently we began to pray to have the snow cease falling. Moving between anxiety and pleasure in our snowbound universe, we hardly knew the next day whether we were sad or perfectly delighted to wake up and discover that the snow had stopped and the sky was clear and blue. What silence, what a world of silence and surrounding snow!

After breakfast the handyman cleared off a place on the veranda and we all stepped out and looked upon an unfamiliar world. How beautiful it was — millions, billions, trillions of tiny rainbow-tinted snow specks turning, twisting, gyrating round and round in the crystal air. All that sparkling brightness, the mass of blinding snow covering the lawns, and the elm trees throwing down their blue and purple shadows, the sound of shovels scraping and the shouts of men clearing the walks and roadways. Could they ever dig us out of such a blizzard? How long would we be closed up in this white prison?

But they dug us out. They cleared the sidewalks and finally Maple Street was opened up. The horsecars began to run, the groceries came and last of all the milkman arrived from Feeding Hills.

Then slowly those vast accumulations of fallen snowflakes, all those mountainous snowdrifts, vanished and there was the sound of rushing waters, the gutters were filled with little rivers. The lawns were islanded with small patches of porous snow; mud sucked the rubbers off our shoes whenever we ran across them. Winter was gone. Buds began to blur the outline of the bare boughs swelling the branches with a brown haze.

The grass appeared. The robins came. Spring was on its way.

And then there came a day of rain and scudding clouds and sunshine when we stood by the old elm stump with Julia Callender; her mother had told her not to play with us unless we asked her, but she'd joined us there — how boastful we were with her — important, while she listened to us with attention as we told her all about the funeral — the many wreaths there were, the quantity of flowers, and such a lot of hacks — and how Rebecca and the boys went in the first hack with our Uncle James and our Aunt Anna — all of them dressed in black. Such a procession! Down the driveway, turning at Maple Street and going slowly, slowly to the cemetery. Had Julia ever had a funeral in *her* house? No, she said honestly, she had not. And then there was her nurse tapping with a thimble at an upper window, and she ran away and left us standing together by the old elm stump.

You remember, Grace, the scudding clouds, the sudden burst of sunshine, that smell of violets and evaporating snow the day our grandmother was carried to the cemetery?

Five

$\mathcal{E}$ACH SPRING that came along was better than the one before. Dandelions studded the grass and then, all of a sudden the lawns were sprinkled over with those tiny three-pronged stars — quaker-ladies was our name for them — fragile, the color of the air, standing up erect on stems almost invisible. How innumerable they were, filling us with a devouring greed — the necessity of getting down upon our knees to gather, to uproot, to possess these little flowers, making them our own and through them the spring.

The spring belonged to us. We lingered outdoors as long as possible, often until the robins had begun their bedtime fluting, that haunting thrush's music, beautiful and sad, and when Mathilda called us how reluctant we were to go indoors.

Everything was at sixes and sevens. Grandma had gone. We could no longer find her in the library sitting beside the fire swinging her slipper on the end of her great toe. We could not find her in her room or in the dining room. Aunt Julia was sitting in her chair at breakfast pouring coffee, pouring the tea at suppertime, carving the roast at dinner. Rebecca and the boys were in their usual places. There was a feeling among us all that we were not so safe and sheltered as before.

The house was full of grown-up people; Aunt Anna and Uncle James were always visiting us, Mrs. Warner and Mrs. Morton stopped in for consultations; plans were being made behind closed doors. Mathilda wept a great deal and said the time had come for her to leave; Aunt Julia, who had figured in our lives as just an old lady with a red face and white hair placing a shawl around our grandmother's shoulders or a rug about her lap, had now become the most important person in the house and we had suddenly discovered that we did not like her and that she did not care for us at all. But here she was and here she intended to stay. She said that Grandma had told her she must be the one to care for us and that she loved us very dearly. She had rheumatism and was cross. The boys despised her and called her awful names behind her back, and Rebecca went her own sweet way paying no attention to anyone. Things went from bad to worse.

Auntie Canfield had been sent from Chestnut Street to help out afternoons. She was worse even than Aunt Julia. They hated each other. Auntie Canfield was a horrid little person with a shrunken body and a shriveled face webbed all over with wrinkles. She had small prying watery eyes and disapproved of every one of us.

One rainy morning something very important happened when we were playing paper dolls upon the stairs, having such fun with our paper people, giving them the names of relatives, inventing their conversations. Without warning Aunt Julia stumbled over us and fell; she picked herself up and declared that she had all but broken her neck, then screamed and raised her hand and slapped us — both of us at the same moment full in the face. And there at the foot of the stairs was our brother James, watching it all.

"You she-devil! You devil you!" he cried. Without another word he turned and ran through the hall, opened the front door and vanished in the rain.

We knew just where he was going and what he intended to do. We lived through every instant of that momentous errand with him; we saw him run down Maple Street in the pelting rain, cross State Street, run up the Chestnut Street hill to the big house, up the stone steps, ring the bell and wait, panting and breathless, until the front door was opened by that awe-inspiring gentleman who always opened the front door at Chestnut Street. Then he dashed right past him into the dining room where Uncle Jim and Aunt Anna and the beautiful young cousins and Chapin and his tutor were breakfasting, looking very rich and formidable. He didn't hesitate a second, but rushed straight to Uncle Jim. Gulping and breathless, he told on Aunt Julia, reciting the shameful story of how she had slapped us while we were playing with our paper dolls, and then, not stopping for interruptions, he said that all of us despised her; blurting everything out, he told how awful she was, the tears streaming down his face. Everyone listened attentively, while Uncle Jim wiped his tears and assured him that he had done right to come and tell his story. When he returned he told us all about it, just what he had said and the promises Uncle Jim and Aunt Anna had given him. We knew that James was our deliverer.

After this, change was in the wind; something great was just about to happen, the thought of which grew too acute for us to bear. Would Aunt Julia be sent away? When was she going? We were sure that the boys were better informed than we were and hung around them trying to discover the secrets that they were holding from us. We couldn't get anything from Rebecca; she went her way alone as usual, shutting herself up with her piano, not inclined to divulge her speculations. But by dint of questioning our brothers, we finally came by information we had not been able to pick up for ourselves. Aunt Julia was really to be dismissed and the guardians were engaged in choosing her successor.

Aunt Julia was very subdued. She appeared to have changed her character altogether. She had stopped her scolding and bossing, and it was often apparent that she had been weeping. Finally the boys, and without our having to tease it from them, came out with the exciting news that the successor had been chosen. Her name was Miss Rogers. They'd gotten much information about her; they told us in the language and accent of Aunt Anna that she was just the proper person for us, that she was "very refined" and, in fact, "a perfect lady." Possessed of all these fascinating facts, we awaited further developments. Her name was Miss Rogers, she was very refined, she was just the proper person for us. When would her arrival be officially announced? We were on tenterhooks. We waited.

Visits from the guardians took on an official rather than a social quality. One day Aunt Julia vanished and on the same afternoon Aunt Anna arrived, unaccompanied by our genial uncle. Her solitary state emphasized the importance of the announcement she was bringing. She gathered us all together in the library and told us solemnly that our Uncle James and she had, after great deliberation, chosen someone to take the place of our grandmother. She hoped, indeed she felt quite sure, that we would learn to love her because she was just the proper person to care for us. She was very kind. She was very refined. Her name, Aunt Anna told us, was Miss Rogers.

Six

WHAT WE DISCOVERED about Miss Rogers on the evening of her arrival was so interesting and the conclusions to which we came so prophetic and accurate that we were well prepared for all that happened in our subsequent relations with her, and none of the irregularities, not to mention the oddities, of life as it went on at Maple Street under her direction, were completely surprising.

Our aunt had planned a welcoming party in which she, our uncle, and the oldest cousins were to take part, and we had been so strung up and so excited all day that our nerves were keyed to the highest pitch of anticipation and response when the great hour arrived.

Miss Rogers had sent her luggage on ahead of her and we had spent most of the afternoon inspecting it. She was to occupy Aunt Julia's room and there we were at six o'clock when we should have been downstairs, trying to extract what we could of the real Miss Rogers from her belongings. She had two trunks, an umbrella, and a bandbox. The bandbox had a queer shape. And was the umbrella, too, a little queer?

"Twinnichen, komm, your brothers and Rebecca are already downstairs," Mathilda called from our room across the hall. "Your hair isn't curled and you must change your dresses."

"All right, we're coming." We ran into our room.

"Naughty girls to go in there again."

"Stop fussing with our curls, Mathilda."

"You must look your best. Tonight is a fine party."

"Yes — we know — they've sent two servants from Chestnut Street. What's the matter with you anyway? You're mixing up our sashes — that's the one for Mary."

"Well, I can't be bothered."

"Never mind. We can tie each other's on the way down."

She dragged us back and tied the proper sash around the right twin's waist. Off we went.

"Be good children," she implored us.

We ran downstairs wondering if it would be possible to behave ourselves in the light of what we were about to experience. By the time we reached the parlor, each girl having poured the burden of her responses into the other's heart, we arrived upon the scene in a highly charged condition. They were all waiting in the south parlor. Every gas jet in the chandelier was lighted. The crystal pendants sparkled. What an affair it was going to be! The cousins had on their party dresses. But why didn't Miss Rogers come?

Uncle Jim was in a sprightly mood; Philip and Rebecca were glum and James was doing nothing to live up to his reputation for helping out in bad moments. Aunt Anna was telling us about Miss Rogers and the way we must behave.

"Remember," she said, "she is your guest and you are her hosts and hostesses."

Uncle Jim advised her not to allow the twins to put beans up their noses. She was much put out and reprimanded him severely, "Remember, Jim, this is a serious occasion."

"I stand corrected, Mamá."

"Miss Rogers," our aunt continued, "is a lady and she will expect gentlemanly and ladylike behavior from you all."

"Isn't that too much to expect of them?" our irrepressible uncle inquired. Seeing from Aunt Anna's expression that he had gone too far, he became suddenly serious and, addressing us all in an admonitory fashion, said that Miss Rogers was used to well-mannered children, that she had lived for three years as governess with the Rand family of New York (as though anybody had ever heard of them), very distinguished people indeed, and that he had it from Mr. and Mrs. Rand themselves that she had not only taught the children their lessons but had turned them from a gang of little rowdies into a crew of well-bred, beautifully brought up boys and girls.

"Does Miss Rogers come from New York?" inquired James.

"Did you know her there?" we asked with eagerness.

"No," said Aunt Anna, answering both questions at once, "she lives in High Street with her mother."

"Here in Springfield?"

"Yes," replied Aunt Anna, becoming still more bewildering. "However, she was born in Litchfield."

"I never knew that, Mamá." Our uncle turned to her. "A very aristocratic little town. One of the oldest in the country."

"Her father was a carriage maker — the Rogers Brothers, I believe, a well-established firm."

"Ah, indeed," said Uncle Jim.

The making of carriages somehow diminishing Miss Rogers's reputation for refinement, we felt considerable disappointment.

But listen! there was the sound of horses' hooves rounding the driveway, carriage wheels. She was coming in a hack.

The conversation had stopped. Everyone listened intently. Miss Rogers was heard coming up the veranda steps accompanied by the driver. We could hear them talking together.

"She will need assistance," suggested our gallant uncle, rising to go to the front door.

"Sit down," ordered Aunt Anna severely, "I have made the arrangements." And to prove the truth of her words, we saw Amelia from Chestnut Street at the front door.

She opened it to let in Miss Rogers and the driver, carrying a satchel and a heavy parcel. Relieving him of both, she bid him good-night, closed the front door, and preceded Miss Rogers upstairs to her bedroom.

We craned our necks for a first glimpse of her. We saw a figure shrouded in a long cape, her face almost entirely concealed by a heavy veil. Waiting for her to prepare herself to come down seemed an eternity. Our impatience grew intolerable. Aunt Anna and Uncle Jim were still discussing Litchfield. Philip and Rebecca were glummer than before, and James again had nothing to contribute to the situation. Listen now — she was coming.

She entered on the tips of her toes walking a little on the bias, ethereal, as though she were about to fly away. She wore a diaphanous gray dress, gray satin slippers of a slightly darker shade — and her hair, arranged in finger curls upon her forehead, was silvery gray. Her face was white and the skin drawn tightly over what appeared to be pale ivory bones. Her deep-set eyes were a peculiar shade of blue that at once communicated sadness and uncertainty. And all this blueness, sadness in the thin pale face declared almost too poignantly a vague perpetual hunger in her heart. As she approached Aunt Anna and Uncle James, she adopted an artificial manner. The voice with which her greetings were effected was a low contralto from which escaped a series of ludicrous little grace notes pitched at a higher key. The pronunciation of each word was carefully, deliberately well-bred, and the effect of all this on the five of us made the effort to suppress our laughter excruciating.

Our uncle, still at the top of his form, began the introductions. "This," he said, laying his hand on Philip's shoulder, "is our bookworm, Philip."

The moment was charged with suspense. Holding our breath we observed our older brother. How would he take to *that?*

He extended his hand and took the contralto greeting with a kind of grim and stoical politeness.

"And this," continued Uncle James, "is Rebecca, our pianist."

She put out her hand and listened rather sulkily while Miss Rogers expatiated upon her own love for the piano, regulating her voice and facial expressions in an attempt to convey her devotion to music.

Now James was stepping up for introduction. Would he fail us again?

"This is our young Lord Chesterfield," said our uncle, proud of his favorite so like him in appearance.

Completely master of the situation, though without knowledge of the character with whom he was compared, James extended his hand and in the name of the entire Miller family welcomed Miss Rogers to our home, and said he hoped that she would be happy here. She appeared enchanted by this beguiling boy and, turning to our guardians, exclaimed that she had never seen anything to equal his "smile and address."

Our turn was coming. The suspense was awful.

"These," our uncle said, "are our little sprigs of Satan, Grace and Mary. I challenge you to tell them apart."

Our desire to perform some perfectly outrageous feat of bad behavior was overwhelming, but we were mercifully saved from immediate banishment by the arrival of Amelia.

"Supper is served."

We followed our uncle into the dining room. Here again everything was arranged with special attention to brightness and festivity. Grandma's Dresden china had been brought out. There were candles and beautiful flowers decorating the table. There was Amelia in her white apron and frilled cap, and even our ancient Hannah was decked out in a stylish cap and apron.

Aunt Anna attended to getting everyone seated, placing herself on Uncle Jim's left and Miss Rogers on his right. She took great pains to separate us, seeing to it that we sat neither next to nor opposite each other, thus depriving us not only of an opportunity to punch and whisper but of the ability to exchange glances as well. The boys she also separated.

Uncle Jim, with his usual gallantry, took a sprig of lemon verbena from the lapel of his coat.

"A whiff of fragrance from our greenhouses at Goshen," he said, offering it to Miss Rogers as he seated himself.

"What an exquisite perfume, Mr. Rumrill," she gushed, delicately sniffing the green leaves.

Messages crossed and re-crossed in the electric air. The boys were carrying on a silent imitation of Miss Rogers, very discreetly and privately, done in pantomime. In spite of Aunt Anna's strategy, our communion was complete. We needed no glances to exchange conjectures and opinions; the best way to corroborate our own surmises was to keep a strict eye upon our brothers.

Miss Rogers was ridiculous but then, poor thing, she must be having an awful time of it and wasn't there anything to be said in her favor? Wasn't there something about her we rather liked?

"Ah," she was saying in her best contralto, "Litchfield is the most aristocratic town. It is where my family settled, Mrs. Rumrill; such stately houses, such ancient elms!"

Watching, listening, we were aware that something very interesting had happened to Miss Rogers. She did not care for our Aunt Anna.

"Yes," replied our aunt, "a fine old town indeed!" and changing the subject abruptly, she said she feared the twins' education had been neglected sadly and that it was time now they had a really suitable governess. How long did she say that she had been with — what was their name? Oh, yes, the Rand family, of course. And of how many children had she been in charge?

"There were three," replied Miss Rogers sadly. "Beautiful children! Two little girls and a boy. I was there five years." She sighed conspicuously. "The severance was difficult." And then, as though throwing herself upon our mercy, she said that she was sure these little twins would take the place of Eleanor and Maude.

The telltale expressions that flitted across her face, the compressed lips, the smile a trifle scornful, the sad blue eyes, and her voice with all those varied intonations reached out as though attempting to ensnare us.

Alarmed lest we be dragged into the meshes of her sentiment, we were enormously relieved when Aunt Anna returned to the subject of teaching. What method does Miss Rogers use and did she teach all the little Rands to speak French?

A jet of almost scornful laughter escaped Miss Rogers's lips. "Method!" she said. "My dear Mrs. Rumrill — I have no method. It is upon the *handling* of my children I depend, and here there are no fixed and standard *methods;* in the words of Shakespeare, 'Necessity is the mother of invention,' and there are so many situations and so many children — such a great variety of little children."

She looked rather desperately around the table to see if there was not one of us to whom she could appeal. Watching her closely we made a firm resolve that we would not look again at James and Philip; we would *not* be influenced by them. We would feel about Miss Rogers the way we wanted to, and we couldn't help feeling sorry for her. Of one thing we were certain — she was going to be a great improvement on Aunt Julia, for all her talk about method and that silly stuff about necessity and invention. What inventions would she try on us? She would have to use a lot of different methods with the Millers.

"What an exquisite soufflé, Mrs. Rumrill."

Why did she use that silly word so often? Look at the way she was holding her fork.

The smell of fresh green leaves and lilacs blew through an open window. The robins on the back lawn were singing the way they do before they go to sleep.

We wondered if she would like it here.

Seven

$\mathcal{H}$ER NAME WAS Desire Aurelia. Desire Aurelia Rogers. The boys called her Auntie Delight and sometimes Auntie Dee. There were times when we could not resist going along with them, giving her their chosen names, putting her through her most entrancing antics, for we knew even better than they her capacity for offering exquisite entertainment.

There was much, however, they never took into account. We felt more about her than they could even dream. She played upon us as on a single instrument. Our nerves were so attuned that the sympathy we gave her accorded perfectly with what, at certain moments, we knew she was undergoing.

Desire — who could have thought up a better name for her? What hopes, what dreams she must have had before she came to live with us. What lovely pictures must have floated and dissolved and built themselves again in that sad and hungry heart. Here everything for which she yearned was waiting for her — to preside as mistress in a gracious, comfortable home and to find five orphaned children in as great need of her as she felt for them — with what tenderness she was prepared to love and cherish them — the beautiful roles that would be hers to assume — a background so perfectly suited to her personality — the visitors she would be called upon to entertain, with her dear children running in and out, always so affectionate and well mannered, helping her to display her accomplishments, not only as a hostess but as the perfect and sorely needed mother of them all.

Think of what she found! First of all, her functions at Maple Street were of a purely domestic and tutorial nature. She had no social life; no visitors came to call; she was never invited out. As to the behavior of the five young orphans — who could have been prepared for that? Poor thing. She stood up bravely to each disappointment. What a false front she managed to put on. She pretended to have every situation well in hand. In her conversations with our guardians she would not admit to any difficulties; Philip was *not*, as they insisted, "unruly, a law unto himself." She greatly enjoyed telling them that she had respect for his "nobility of mind," and that the way to manage him was not to manage him at all. James, who actually was the instigator of most of the lawlessness, she continued to maintain, was, with his "smile and address," no trouble at all. Rebecca was perhaps "not easy to understand," but they must give her time to win her confidence. As for us, she was reluctant to go into much discussion, having already begun to assume that we were her special province and possession.

In spite of the inventions of which she had so arrogantly boasted, none was applied with the slightest success. One crisis seemed to follow another. Our brothers were far too old to spank; perhaps she could have thrashed them, but imagine the refined Miss Rogers letting down the trousers of those unruly boys. She could deprive them of their weekly stipend; she could send them to their rooms until such time as they wished to make apologies. On occasions, driven to the verge of desperation, she would very reluctantly (for she knew it was an admission of defeat) employ a terrifying threat, "I will report you to your Uncle James!" Of course, they knew that she would never think of doing such a thing; *her* ordeal in going to our unpredictable uncle would far exceed any punishment he might inflict on them.

In her dealings with us, Aunt Anna was the highest court of justice. "Your Aunt Anna will hear of this!" was an empty threat, for we were completely aware of how she dreaded the least association with our overpowering aunt. We knew well that even our worst behavior would never reach her ears.

The hostility toward Aunt Anna, of which we had been acutely conscious on the evening of her arrival, grew more and more noticeable. She could not bear her. Every slight to which she felt herself subjected, her exclusion from society, her inferior position, she laid at Aunt Anna's door. This feeling became so intense that it was impossible for her to contain it. It was always escaping her. Scorn, sarcasm, pleasure in a sense of her own superiority, and at times undisguised malice flitted across her face, twitching the muscles of her cheeks, curling her lip.

Toward our uncle her feelings were not so intense, but in talking of him it gave her pleasure to let us know that she was well aware of his position in relationship to our aunt. "Your uncle supervises the expenditures at Maple Street, but it is your Aunt Anna who stands behind his orders and reprimands. Where the money is, *there* is the authority. The almighty dollar speaks."

She was in dread of having to confront Uncle Jim, though she greatly enjoyed indulging in allusions to his vanity, his elegances of dress, and the frivolities of his behavior. In short, she never failed to let us know that she regarded him as a very ridiculous little gentleman. The monthly sessions when he came to go over the accounts became the most dreaded of all her confrontations. Days before them she became worried and distracted and would sit up late into the night going over her books and trying to make the accounts come out right. Who could expect her, with the miserable pittance allowed, to run this house and dress and feed five children, to say nothing of keeping up appearances? How deeply we felt for her, and when the awful day arrived and she was closeted with him for hours in the library, we used to wait for her outside the door, anxious and imagining everything that she was going through. When she finally emerged, wan and pale, she looked as though she had been dealt a physical injury.

Drastic changes occurred. Mathilda departed. Grandma's ancient Hannah left, to be followed by such a procession of Hannahs, Noras, Ellens, and Bridgets that it is impossible to remember when they came and why they vanished. We were usually short of either a waitress or a cook and frequently of both. Miss Rogers's sorrowful explanations for these calamities being invariably the same — our aunt expected too much of her — a certain style at least, a fitting decency must be maintained.

She loved the place and grieved continually about the way it had been allowed to go to rack and ruin. Presently, she hit upon a brilliant solution for bringing it back to something of its old order by installing Patrick Sullivan. Though only on occasion in a state of total intoxication, he was always tipsy. His figure was bent, his coat tattered. His face, red and round and foolish, though never graced with a full growth of whiskers, was chronically unshaven, the abundant crop of stiff white bristles contributing greatly to his thoroughly disreputable appearance. He was to have the little yellow house at the foot of the bankings, and for the smallest possible wage was to perform all kinds of miracles in restoring the grounds and gardens, to say nothing of being general handyman about the house. He did his best to prune the trees, resurrect the asparagus bed, and make the roses bloom again, as well as assisting in unexpected emergencies. He followed Miss Rogers around like a drunken Caliban. Between them there existed a very peculiar relationship. He regarded her as a "foine lady, a very foine lady indeed," and gave her his entire besotted devotion; while she, never losing her faith in his abilities and enjoying the opportunities he so frequently gave her to lecture and upbraid and graciously forgive, derived great comfort and sustenance from his unfailing regard for her. "Yes, Miss Ratchers. No, Miss Ratchers, and what should I be doing now?"

Her attempts to impose total abstinence upon him met with no success, but nonetheless he remained during her entire stay at Maple Street, a permanent ornament to our household.

Eight

WHEN WE BECAME acclimated to Miss Rogers, her prejudices and pronouncements and her surprising innovations, it was as though a strong wind had moved through our heart and mind and almost but not quite blown away all memories of the time when our gentle grandmother had presided over us at Maple Street.

A certain order of events became established. Sundays were ritual affairs — church in the morning; after church on alternate Sundays, dinner at Chestnut Street, and on the following week the relatives dining with us. Christmas came and Easter and the spring, then early summer when the relatives departed for their farm on Goshen Point, leaving Miss Rogers to hold the reins alone; our departure for the yearly visit to the farm, those long six weeks beside the sea, the difficult readjustment to the elegances of life and what Miss Rogers called, "overindulgence in the fleshpots of Egypt," our delight in the wide seascapes and the far horizon, the fragrance of the meadows, the scent of blended pollens and fresh salt breezes; our return to Maple Street for the late summer days, the song of katydids swinging from bough to bough among the elm trees, the ripening fruits upon the bankings, the familiar autumn joys and after that the first frost and the first fall of snow — the anticipation of Christmas.

The boys and Rebecca went to school, leaving us much more than they the victims of Miss Rogers's inventions and experiments; our education was left entirely in her hands. We were supposed to keep regular school hours in her bedroom every morning. Two small tables were installed; on each of these, neatly laid out, was a slate and a slate pencil, a sponge to clean the slate, and a Holy Bible. The school hours were supposed to last from nine to twelve but they were always being interrupted — it might be the cook giving notice in the kitchen, or Patrick needing supervision in the garden or the cellar, or the sudden ringing of the doorbell and Miss Rogers being called away to interview a policeman — did the Miller boys live here? Windows had been broken on Maple Street, a lamppost had been taken down and carried off. What with the time she had to spend adjusting all these various matters, it was not unusual for her to find us upon her return in the midst of one of our battles.

If she needed to be taught that, where one of us was implicated, there to exactly the same degree the other one was implicated too, she should have learned it on these occasions. The subject of our quarrels might differ, but invariably they were an unconscious attempt to establish a separate identity. One of us would claim the honor of inventing some crazy phrase or the credit for the performance of some mad act sprung directly from our identical sense of the ridiculous, and the other would assert that it had been the invention of *her* brain. In the grip and throes of our oneness, not knowing who had said what or who was hitting whom, we erupted in a spontaneous combustion —

"I said it first."

"You did not. *I* did."

"*I* thought of 'Monkey Black Bat.' *I* invented it."

Miss Rogers had one method of dealing with these disgraceful fights. Assuming a calm angelic expression, she would begin to intone the thirteenth chapter of Corinthians, bidding us repeat the healing words:

"Love suffereth long and is kind . . ."

". . . she's biting me, Miss Rogers . . ."

". . . Mary scratched my arm . . ."

"Vaunteth not itself, is not puffed up . . ."

". . . she's biting my wrist . . ."

". . . she scratched my lip . . ."

". . . *I* said 'Hack of the Karoussi' . . ."

". . . You did not. *I* invented it . . ."

". . . You're a liar . . ."

". . . I am not. *You* are . . ."

". . . *Whether there be prophecies, they shall fail, whether there be tongues they shall cease . . . for we know in part, and we prophesy in part. But when that which is perfect is come, then that which is in part shall be done away. . . ."*

Sniffling, kicking, not certain who had scratched or bitten whom, we tried to join with her in the repetition of the all-too-familiar words. Almost hypnotized by the modulation of her voice and the music and rhythms of the incomprehensible words, we felt our anger subsiding. The tempest was over as suddenly as it had begun. Miss Rogers was convinced that her method had succeeded.

For dealing with more difficult displays of temper when our conjoined wrath was leveled not against ourselves but against her, Miss Rogers resorted to the most spectacular of all her experiments — the ice-cold bath. To get us both into the bathroom, it was necessary to call in Patrick Sullivan. When this was achieved, the door was locked. Miss Rogers turned on the cold water full force. Patrick grabbed one twin, she grabbed the other. They struggled to undress us while we screamed and kicked and violently resisted. We would have killed them if we could, but they overpowered us. We were immersed. We called them unmentionable names. We drenched them with handfuls of water. Gasping, shivering, very nearly drowning in our sobs, we were forced to yield.

"Now you're getting cooler — now you're calming down," Miss Rogers assured us as she emptied the sponge over our shivering bodies. Behind her Patrick Sullivan, wet and dripping from his whiskers to his ragged trousers, confusedly inquired, "And what should I be doing next, Miss Ratchers?"

"Keep them from jumping out! It won't be long now, Patrick. They're cooling off, they're calming down."

"Sure, Miss Ratchers, sure."

There were times when each one of us had gone so far into entering not only the other's heart and mind, but into her actual bodily mechanism, that we were both acutely aware that once our bad behavior had been set in motion, nothing on earth could have stopped one from going on to the end of the act until the other's responding reflexes had, so to speak, run down. Shuddering and exhausted, completely worn out, we had certainly calmed down and were quite ready to give up the struggle.

"There, there, didn't I tell you? See how beautifully it worked." Miss Rogers, weary but triumphant, dismissed Patrick and assisted us, blue and with chattering teeth, to step out of the bathtub, tenderly assuring us that to administer her method had given her far more pain than she had given us. She enveloped us in all her love. We were not only docile, we were penitent and made no objections to being put to bed. Indeed, we were grateful for an opportunity to recover our strength. We asked her to forgive us for wanting to kill her.

Fatigued and lying side by side between the cool white sheets, the tides of forgiveness ran so strong that we were overcome with love. We felt cleansed of hatred and rebellion and ready to receive the genial flow of life and joy that had been so rudely interrupted; we experienced measureless gratitude for being restored to our usual self.

Through the open window came the fragrance of young green growths. The robins were singing that music which had become the very theme song of our life at Maple Street. We heard the voices of the boys as they ran across the lawn. A familiar piece of music that Rebecca had already freighted for us with memories and associations came floating up from the south parlor.

The front door slammed. The boys had come in. Life was continuing as usual.

Nine

_As_ TIME WENT ON, life at Maple Street became more and more anarchic. Miss Rogers's attempts at discipline were in vain. Our brothers took the law into their hands and made insubordination the order of the day. "I won't. Who are you to order me around?" was the language to which she had become accustomed, knowing well that none of the threats or the punishments she held above their heads were of the slightest avail and that she might declare a hundred times that she would report them to their Uncle James, but that these were empty words. The relatives were not aware of what was going on behind their backs, since we certainly had no intention of carrying tales to Chestnut Street and when in their presence the behavior of us all was reasonably good. We managed to convince them of this with a variety of stock phrases like little pieces learned by heart, all of which they took as a measure of our usual good manners.

What scenes we witnessed. What sudden and unexpected fights. What violence. What bloodshed.

Fascinated, yet filled with consternation, we looked on. How far was it possible that we could go and how long could we stand the strain? Grace and I had become inured to the shock and jar of habitual anarchy; we did not have to compare our reactions since we knew they were the same — sympathy for Miss Rogers, an almost demonic delight in lawlessness, and at the same time an unconscious aching need for stability.

The dining room was the principal arena. One memorable morning at breakfast when everything was serene, Miss Rogers was drinking her coffee, enjoying the charming scene, surrounded by her five handsome children. She looked with approval upon us all. Philip leaned casually toward Rebecca, extended his fork and filched a piece of bacon from her plate.

"My food is my own when it's given me," she cried indignantly.

Repeating her laughable words, he mocked her with them.

Rebecca began to cry.

"You must not mock your sister," Miss Rogers rebuked. At which, and to everyone's amazement, Philip flung his tumblerful of water directly into her astonished face.

Surely this merited the severest measures. We waited for what was coming next. Miss Rogers sat there, her gray curls plastered to her brow, water streaming down her cheeks protesting, "Philip — why Philip — ." That was all. Philip continued with his breakfast, thoroughly enjoying himself.

This, though surprising indeed and furnishing us with a model of insolence and audacity, which was hardly to be surpassed, had a touch of novelty that gave us a certain pleasure and did not cause us the fear and trembling that we experienced during the hair-raising fights that often broke out between the boys. What we always regarded as the worst of these started very suddenly.

What was it all about? They were discussing a football game; James said something about someone's fumbling a ball. Philip contradicted, "He didn't fumble it. He *caught* it." James insisted, "He *fumbled* it," and then without further argument Philip hurled his plate across the table; it broke on James's chin, cutting him badly. Up sprang James and they were at each other tooth and nail. Nobody could stop them. The table between the windows was turned over. Everything was smashed to smithereens. Blood streamed; James's nose was bleeding. The fight continued.

"They're killing each other, Miss Rogers — Philip's murdered James!" we screamed. Stopping our ears we rushed out of the room, through the hall out of the front door, still screaming, *"Murder — murder — Philip's murdered James!"*

Violence was almost an everyday occurrence. Violence that Miss Rogers could not handle. All her methods with these incorrigible boys had failed, but with us, assisted by St. Paul and Patrick Sullivan, she felt herself triumphant and successful. It was to us she turned for understanding and fulfillment, playing upon our sympathy out of her knowledge of the pity we gave her in all her trials. Not entirely aware of the extent to which she exploited our feelings for her, but unable to escape from the net she had so gradually drawn around us, we became the victim of her devouring need.

We'd almost stopped going along with the boys, but on the rare occasions when she came down to supper arrayed in that same gray dress in which she had made her first appearance, full of airs and graces, we would inveigle her into the south parlor.

"Oh, Miss Rogers," we would plead, "won't you please sing us our favorite song — you know, the beautiful one about the sunset and the sea?"

Happy to give us pleasure, she would seat herself at the piano and, throwing back her head and placing her long aristocratic fingers on the keys, she would tune her usual contralto to an incredible falsetto and incredibly enunciating every word give us her little song.

"Oh my, oh me, the sunset is the sea — "

When she had finished, suppressing with the utmost difficulty the laughter that convulsed us we exclaimed, "You sang it beautifully, Miss Rogers; and now won't you please sing the lullaby we love so much?"

Smiling and nodding assent she would begin again:

"Sleep, baby, sleep — Thy father watcheth the sheep —
Thy mother is shaking the dreamland tree
When down falls a little dream on thee."

How many little dreams had fallen and shattered around her in this the latest home of that long and unrequited dream — her life?

Ten

COME, IT IS MAY. The violets are out. Let us find them. Across the veranda, over the lawn, filled with delight in the fragrance and freshness of morning we run to our garden of moss under the oak trees close to the bankings. Here we find what we expected — small ferns emerging like gnomes with wooly caps, little toadstools just sprung up — look! all these bright specks of orange and red and green, flowers of the moss erect on stems that nobody can see, and encroaching on the moss our violets, the tiny white ones on their stunted stems, too short and small to make into a bunch but let us pick a few just for the sheer delight in smelling them. Look how perfect and precise they are, and round their throats the rim of gold, the delicate dark blue pencilings above. Now take a long, long whiff. What bliss escapes upon the breath we draw in to capture it. Take another breath. Heavenly fragrance.

But we must be off now. There are other violets we must find. Pell-mell down the first bank to the terrace below. Here are the beautiful, the purple long-stemmed ones — enormous. Sit down beside me. The grass is wet. Unseen fingers twist and turn the facets of a thousand dewdrops toward the sun. Emeralds and sapphires and rubies are rolling in the grass. Dip into the wetness. Be careful to find the end of each stem before you pick it. Oh, here's a beauty. Such a long one. An oriole sings in the pear tree above us. The petals of pear blossoms tremble in the grass. Oh, look what a bunch I've picked — "But my bunch is larger than yours . . ." We bury our face in the cool wet flowers.

It is June. A warm night after supper. Hundreds of fireflies are lighting their lamps and putting them out in the blue summer dark. Up in the air in the branches of the elm trees above the lawn they are flitting and sparking and are there two girls floating, running, lifting up their arms to catch the sparks; or is there one? And which of us has captured this curious flickering creature? Are Grace's fingers illuminated by this cool phosphorescence or is it I who have caught our little captive, lighting, extinguishing his lamp in my hand?

It is October. The light so strong that gnats and midges and the wings of birds are silver bright, and threads the spiders spin shine like spun glass in the autumnal air. Down on the bankings the fruits are ripe. As we sit here in the long untended grass, all our senses are assailed at once. The air is filled with a glut of smells; the sun ripens the apples and pears and draws out the richer smell of fruits already fallen to the ground. Incessant the hum of bees and hornets as they swarm around the rotting pears, demolishing, eating them down to the core. In the arbors the grapes hang heavy on the vines and here their perfume is so warm and sweet it makes a vintage of its own. We devour the purple clusters. The ground is strewn with their blue-black skins and the small translucent pulps that we spit out as we suck the wine of the grapes to the very dregs. Crickets chirp. A solitary robin sings.

Eleven

Now I lay me down to sleep,
I pray the Lord my soul to keep.
If I should die before I wake,
I pray the Lord my soul to take.

*E*VERY NIGHT WE were admonished to kneel
down beside each other, our hands folded and our elbows on
the bed, and say in unison this accustomed prayer. We were
generally so sleepy that the words were only a prelude to tum-
bling into bed and going fast asleep. But sometimes they remained in our mind as matter for contemplation. The first
thing that seemed wrong was that we were saying, "If *I*
should die before *I* wake," instead of "we." Was one of us
likely to die before the other? This was impossible to contemplate. Moreover, what was this thing in our possession
that the Lord might choose to take or keep? What was a soul?
It seemed to have something to do with God. We placed it in
his keeping while we slept and if we died before we woke, we
prayed that he would take it. Where? Where would he take
our soul? To heaven, of course, which as everybody knew was

where he lived. And often when we lay in bed and looked up at all the stars we could feel him — we were together underneath the shining sky and we knew that he was with us. Was this knowledge not related to that happiness that sometimes, when we were out of doors, almost without our knowing it had happened, made us aware that God was most mysteriously present?

Religion as expounded to us by our elders was full of contradictions. Miss Rogers was an Episcopalian; she believed in a Trinitarian God; the guardians were Unitarians. To confuse God so bewilderingly with Jesus and the Holy Ghost bereft him of his unique and terrifying power. Was Carlo Dolci's Infant whom we saw above the mantelpiece in the south parlor the selfsame child whose birth we celebrated at Christmas? And was he, placed beneath the Christmas tree in his cradle, surrounded by the camels and the cows and sheep and all the kneeling wise men, the same Almighty God who made the earth and sea and all that is in them? It was lovely to believe that there had once been born upon the earth a child who grew in wisdom till all the things he said when he was grown had now become the rules by which we all were taught the ways of love and kindness. But when Miss Rogers said he had been begotten by the Holy Ghost and born of the Virgin Mary, we were unable to fit these apparitions into our understanding.

We went every Sunday to the Unitarian Church. Its Gothic interior was grave and impressive. Immediately upon entering we were assailed by a sepulchral smell that, mingling with the sound of the organ, seemed to disturb our inner equilibrium. Weights changed and balances shifted as, inundated by the resonant voluntary, we walked down the aisle. The march was brief and the emotion strange and powerful. A sense of being flooded by — what was it? Fear? Exaltation?

Mr. Cookson was ascending the pulpit stairs. Our aunt, though occupied in praying, separated us and we sat one on either side of her. When our aunt prayed, we were conscious that she was asking God to give her strength to meet her cares and responsibilities and that the greatest of these was the Miller children. Her righteousness and piety oppressed us. It was difficult through the long service to sustain so much religion; the prayers, the readings of the lessons, the getting up and sitting down never knowing whether or not to bow our heads. But nonetheless the church itself with its solemn beauty, its well-proportioned aisles, the long Gothic windows, imposed upon us a kind of private reverence. There was one window executed in richly colored glass that affected us particularly. Jesus was depicted walking in the grass beside a brook. He was robed in a long mantle of ruby red and carried a shepherd's crook. In his arms were two young lambs; three larger lambs were cropping the grass. The living waters flowing at his feet were blue and little flowers bright as gems were shining on the banks. Beneath this window was inscribed on a brass plate:

IN MEMORY OF CHARLES PHILIP AND GRACE RUMRILL MILLER, the dates of their birth and death below.

This window was just behind us on the other side of the church and by craning our necks we were able to look at it, conscious of our orphaned condition and wondering how many members of the congregation guessed that the five lambs represented the Miller children.

In spite of the discomfort, the fidgets and the boredom, and the intolerable length of Mr. Cookson's sermon, the shifts and changes in our spiritual equilibrium contributed more than a little to the growing realization that we were indeed in the possession of a soul.

We looked forward to the singing of the hymns. There were some with which we were well acquainted and when these were sung we were delighted. "Rock of Ages, cleft for me, let me hide myself in thee," induced in us a delicious melancholy. "Jerusalem the Golden" and "Jerusalem My Happy Home" were especially dear to us. When we sang, "Thy gardens and thy goodly walks forevermore are green," we felt as much at home in heaven as on the lawns and bankings at Maple Street. The performance that we enjoyed the most was the sudden appearance in the choir loft above the pulpit of Miss Annie Bailey, Mr. Samuel Chapin, Miss Lucie Pynchon, and Mr. Theodore Pratt. Tilting their heads as though listening too intently to one another, they harmonized their voices, accompanied by the great sonorous organ. It was surprising to discover within ourselves instruments — stops and strings on which unseen fingers seemed to play, producing music at times so full of sadness that we learned sorrow was composed of exquisite vibrations to be deliciously enjoyed. Then clouds burst asunder, trumpets and angels proclaimed the glory of God and the beauty of the world and we were lifted to bright realms of joy. Meanwhile, the sun, having reached our window, was illuminating Jesus' red mantle and in a pew across the way on the shoulders of Miss Maria Foote a large crimson stain was quivering.

Finally Mr. Cookson's sermon was over. The contribution boxes had been passed, the last hymn sung, the benediction pronounced. The relief of it. The joy of breathing fresh air with the wide blue sky above us and no more church until next Sunday.

Twelve

O N T H E S U N D A Y S when we dined at Chestnut Street, Miss Rogers expected us to wait for her at the Episcopal Church, which was on the way. The boys and Rebecca would go ahead and Uncle Jim and Aunt Anna drove home as usual. We crossed State Street and climbed the Chestnut Street hill. At the top was Miss Rogers's church. Although she was invited, she often declared she would not join us. We always managed to persuade her to come. Fresh from her Trinitarian devotions, she was ready to criticize the faith to which we had just been exposed.

"Unitarianism! What kind of religion is that? Does Christ take any part in it? A very good man indeed," she mocked, "so was Socrates for that matter — " She went on until we reached Aunt Anna's gate, giving us the benefit of arguments she would hardly have dared voice to our guardians.

The interval between our arrival and the announcement of dinner was the most difficult for her; having prepared for the ordeal, she outdid herself. She greeted our aunt effusively, "Such a pleasure to see you in your own home, my dear Mrs. Rumrill — and what a beautiful home it is."

Uncle Jim, breaking in, shook her hand with his usual joviality. "I see you have assembled your troop."

"They are all here. I hope their behavior will not disgrace me," she said facetiously. "After all, the members of your *other* household are not accustomed to the amenities required here." Her complimentary and pointed remarks accompanied by much unnecessary laughter fell on deaf ears. The formalities accomplished, our aunt and uncle turned their attention to us, consigning her to complete oblivion. By the time dinner was announced she was sufficiently crushed to subside into comparative silence.

There were thirteen at the table counting Chapin's tutor and Auntie Canfield. The amount of attention paid to the latter was the bitterest pill Miss Rogers had to swallow. Auntie Canfield had been nurse to all the Rumrill children and was now, given the title of housekeeper, almost a member of the family. Her eccentricities had become family possessions. She was petted and spoiled and given license to say whatever she pleased.

Mr. Dow, latest of the tutors, was, according to Auntie Canfield's standards, of as little importance as Miss Rogers. She could tolerate neither one nor the other, being of the opinion that the family she had served so long demeaned themselves by having at their table people who were scarcely above the level of hired help.

Though the table was beautifully decorated and the food far more delicious than anything we ever had at Maple Street, we were not completely able to enjoy it. We were so much in awe of the butler that we could never muster enough courage to take the second helping, but far more distressing was the social drama going on around us. Auntie Canfield, the little lady so self-important sitting there in her black bombazine trimmed all over with dangling beads, noticed that Philip was gobbling his food and remarked, "Dear me Suz — in *this* household the Rumrill children were taught better. I never seen such works!"

Mr. Dow, fully aware of the animosities and favoritisms involved, was amused by all that was going on and included us in his enjoyment by a surreptitious wink. Miss Rogers, left out entirely, was doing her best to establish a connection with him, whom she regarded as the only one at the table capable of appreciating her. "You have been given a compliment, Mr. Dow," she said, looking disdainfully at Auntie Canfield.

Though Miss Rogers found the Sunday dinners at Chestnut Street unendurable, she had no idea of how acutely we shared her discomfiture.

After dinner, in the parlor the ensuing session followed an invariable pattern. Coffee was served and Miss Rogers had her opportunity to express herself. Never had she tasted such delicious after-dinner coffee. Where had the cook learned her art? She sipped it in a state approaching ecstasy, crooking her finger gracefully.

Music followed: Cousin Rebecca and our own Rebecca playing duets together. Miss Rogers had another opportunity to make her presence known by applauding enthusiastically — "Bravo, well done."

It was a relief to say good-bye to Chestnut Street and be on our way; one on either side of her we started off. Our joy in being out, especially in springtime under the budding trees and in our new spring hats and coats, as though we too were putting forth our buds and flowers, was so extreme that we must let go her hand and take a run and skip ahead. Skip to the right, skip to the left, and be careful not to step upon the cracks. Arriving at Maple Street, when we first saw the green lawns and the yellow house we felt an equal joy with Miss Rogers, for she loved the place just as we did. Why this should be we often wondered.

The Sundays when the relatives came to us offered a different situation altogether. Miss Rogers was the hostess and the greater part of the week was spent in planning for the occasion. How many would be likely to arrive? The young ladies were often away visiting friends; Chapin and his tutor were frequently exempted; Auntie Canfield, she reminded herself with pleasure, was automatically to be excluded. The important question — would extra leaves in the dining-room table be needed? — she irritably addressed to us. "Your aunt never lets me know who is coming until the last minute."

Every day she counted the napkins and the tablecloths, uncertain as to whether the larger or the smaller would be required — in any event all the silver had to be carefully polished. She was perpetually changing the menu and wondering if she could persuade the presiding Hannah or Maria to wear a ruffled cap and apron.

When we were all finally seated around our much extended dining-room table, Miss Rogers, doing her best to play the role of hostess while her mind was full of apprehension about the progress of the ceremony that was so precariously going on, looked to us the very image of despair. Uncle Jim carved. It was not only apparent that the carving knife was dull but that he looked with suspicion on the size of the leg of lamb or the roast of beef. "A gargantuan feast you are offering us, Miss Rogers," he would often exclaim, putting into his voice a slight note of censure at her extravagance. As the meal proceeded in a pathetic attempt to imitate the Chestnut

Street repasts, entree following roast, salad following entree, and an elaborate dessert finishing it all off, it was clear that our aunt and uncle would rather have been served a humble meal of corned beef and cabbage with baked apples for dessert, than to see the sum total of these pretentious dinners added to the other items on the monthly budget.

Everything was poorly cooked and badly served and Miss Rogers continued to apologize throughout the meal. When after-dinner coffee was finally brought into the south parlor on a heavy silver tray and poured into Grandma's best cups, she never failed to lament the weak, tepid brew that could hardly match the excellence of that provided by our aunt.

When it was all over, everybody gave a sigh of great relief. We were happy to be at ease in our own home again.

Thirteen

We used to question Miss Rogers about her mother, of course, we knew she had one and that she lived on High Street — our aunt had said so. She always disappeared one afternoon a week and it was not long before we knew where she was going.

"How old is your mother?" we would ask. "Why don't you live with her instead of us?"

Her answers were never very satisfactory and she enjoyed throwing a veil of mystery around the subject. She would disappear every week saying that she was entitled to her afternoon off.

"Won't you take us with you, Miss Rogers? We'd like to see your mother. Do you tell her about us and what awful children we are?"

Miss Rogers said her mother knew all about us.

"Well, then she must be dying to see us."

She was not very strong, it seemed, and must be protected.

"Wouldn't she enjoy a visit from us someday when she was feeling very well?"

Miss Rogers hesitated. "Perhaps," she said.

"Does anyone take care of her?"

"I provide," Miss Rogers answered.

It was a long time later and after a great deal of teasing that she finally consented to take us along with her. Filled with curiosity, we climbed the High Street hill remarking the smallness of the houses and wondering in which one of these Miss Rogers's mother lived. Near the top of the hill the houses were set above a bank and it was necessary to climb up some rough-hewn wooden steps to reach them. Mrs. Rogers lived in the smallest and highest of them all. Her house looked exactly like a bird cage hung among the branches of the over-arching trees and it was impossible not to exclaim, "What a funny place to live in!"

We crossed a veranda with an ornamental lattice. On entering we were startled to discover not only an old lady in a wheel chair but an elderly gentleman in attendance.

In a somewhat gruesome way Mrs. Rogers resembled her daughter. The skeletal structure of her face was the same, but the skin that covered it was dry and brown with age. And in her ancient features was displayed all the haughtiness and pride with which we were already familiar. Her attempt at eloquence of speech was impaired by her cracked and tremulous voice, which had a way of flying off into little shrieks and cackles.

We were much surprised to learn that the elderly gentleman was Miss Rogers's brother Manley; he had the same gaunt, high-cheeked countenance as Desire and his mother, but without a shred of their arrogance and pride. He was humble and unassertive; the only time he spoke was to say,

"Yes, Mother," or "As you say, Dee."

Did Manley do the cooking and the housework and put his mother to bed, we wondered?

In spite of the surroundings, Miss Rogers and her mother did their best to maintain their aristocratic pretensions. Manley was required to fetch various objects of importance to show us. Perhaps we would be interested in seeing a first edition of Washington Irving's *Alhambra?* — or a letter written by Chief Justice Marshall and signed by his own hand? Then there was a daguerreotype of Governor Wolcott, who was a cousin of Desire's great-great-uncle.

We did our best to respond with some enthusiasm to these dusty curios but were really occupied in wondering about Manley.

After this we accompanied Miss Rogers quite frequently on her visits to the bird cage. Having once exposed us she began to talk more and more of her mother. Out of her love for her she attempted to transform this ghoulish old figure into a great lady, but she was never willing to satisfy our curiosity about Manley. Actually, what she succeeded in doing was to strengthen our pity and our need to protect her.

The weekly visits continued. In time Mrs. Rogers became a part of all the other burdens we had taken on with our dear Desire. When after a severe cold she came down with pneumonia, Miss Rogers went every day to High Street. In response to our inquiries about her mother's condition, Miss Rogers's mood, sorrowful and resigned, and her avowals of faith in God and religion, served to convey to us the certainty that Mrs. Rogers was about to die.

She did not weep but maintained until after the funeral a state of stoic religious calm in which she expected us to join. She spoke of the beauty that death had imparted and wanted us to see her mother one last time. On a sudden impulse we ran down the bankings and picked a large bunch of violets.

It touched us very much to see that these had been placed in her mother's hands. Overcoming our horror, and each mustering whatever courage the other possessed, we stood beside the coffin and took a long last look at the old lady. We found no beauty in the familiar features but a stillness there, a final gathering up of all her pride and determination into an awful mold.

This presence remained with us, visiting us seldom in the daytime but beginning more and more to haunt our nights. It was not so much Mrs. Rogers herself, but that her death had gathered round it the accumulated terrors that had sub-terraneously pursued us since those early days when Philip's intolerable cry of "CHOLERA!" had set in motion a brood of nameless fears and apprehensions. When these dreams took on the quality of nightmares, and terror broke through sleep fusing itself into our being, we were invaded by overwhelming dread. Of what unimaginable knowledge could it have been composed?

After we had endured this condition as long as was hu-manly possible, there came an instant when we both arose, and who was the first to step out of bed and start upon our journey toward deliverance and which girl was following which we never knew.

We had not far to go. But when we had to pass the dreaded western window our courage faltered. Elm trees tapped upon the pane, boughs swung out into the dark, voices, whispers, terrible assertions reached out to seize and petrify us. Could we achieve the awful passage? There was a goal we must reach: a few steps more, across the threshold and into Miss Rogers's bed. There in perfect safety the knowledge that we feared withdrew.

Fourteen

ONE WINTER, I can't remember which, a strange thing occurred. I had an experience in which Grace took no part. I went through it entirely alone. I remember plainly how it started. It was a winter afternoon and we were out with our sleds. The snow was melting and rain was in the air. The edges of our coats and our mittens and coat sleeves were soaking wet; my teeth were chattering and I was cold; I had a sharp pain between my shoulders of which I complained bitterly. Finally, I said that I was going in. Grace followed me and, when we found Miss Rogers, said, "Mary's feeling awful. She doesn't want to slide or anything."

Miss Rogers felt my forehead and took my temperature; she sent immediately for the doctor. I was put to bed in Grandma Rumrill's bedroom.

From the moment I touched the mattress and shivered at the impact of the cool linen sheets I was conscious only of my bodily sensations. I lay there in my solitary bed; that presence which had always certified my own existence had vanished completely. I was alone. Lifted slowly, my body growing larger and larger and then shrinking, growing very small and smaller still, I wondered where I was. The little aunts, Sarah, Laura and Rebecca, had left their frames and were beckoning me to follow them. Off we floated together, farther and farther away. Whether I attempted to resist I was unable to tell, for floating still I realized I was returning and that the little aunts had ceased to beckon. At undetermined intervals I saw a figure dressed in white, a cap upon her head, hovering over me; sometimes Dr. Stewart was beside me asking questions, trying to make me tell him how I felt. I tried to tell Miss Rogers or the nurse or the doctor that it hurt to take a breath and how I wished the pain would stop. And then I gave up trying to make anyone understand and began again to follow the little aunts, rising, carried off beyond reach — beyond all sense of human touch or voice or admonition.

The place in which I floated swallowed nights and days; it would be easy to make no effort to return — was I drifting? was I sinking? was I rising? was I falling? Here nothing was demanded of me but to keep on floating within this endless void, the loneliness of which grew more and more appalling. I must try by some tremendous effort to pull myself back upon the mattress where I could feel the weight of my own body.

Fatigued beyond endurance I lay weightless no longer, sapped of all energy, sinking into abysses of soft and comfortable sleep.

When I woke from what must have been a long and refreshing sleep the pain had gone. I lay in Grandma Rumrill's bed and there in their frames were Sarah, Laura and Rebecca.

Miss Rogers was standing over me and the nurse was at the window looking at the thermometer. I told them I had been asleep and that the pain between my shoulders had stopped. I did not ask for Grace but lay there rejoicing in my comfortable single self.

The next day Grace came in to see me. She rushed up to the bed and with explosive joy exclaimed, "Oh Mary, you are better. It has been terrible without you."

I looked into the face that had always reflected everything that I was feeling and knew for the first time that I had had an experience that set me quite apart from her in its importance.

"Grace," I said, without disguising the great pride I felt, "I very nearly died."

She was deeply impressed. "I know you did," she answered, as though she held me in a kind of awe.

Accepting my claim to individual honor I boastfully repeated, "I nearly died."

I lived for some time as a separate being; my convalescence awarded me special privileges and distinctions. When Miss Rogers presented me with a brand new ten-dollar bill in honor of my illness and recovery, Grace did not feel that the enormous fortune into which I had just come was one in which she should share. I felt that I should offer her half but my unnatural pleasure in owning it alone deterred me. I put the bill beneath my pillow and each time I awoke I made certain it was still there. During my convalescence we discussed endlessly what I was to buy with it. We finally hit upon a silver hairbrush.

When I was well enough, we went to all the jewelers in town. Many silver brushes were laid out for our inspection. At last we chose a large brush, the back embossed with silver flowers and with an unadorned circle in the center for a monogram to be engraved. We took a long time selecting the design for the entwined letters — M.B.M.

The brush with its fine monogram arrived. Together we took it up to our room and placed it on the bureau — *my* brush with my initials. I told Grace she might use it whenever she wanted to; she was grateful but never did so, nor did I use it myself, preferring the ordinary wooden-back one that had always been regarded as "ours together." The great silver object remained a magnificent ornament in the center of our bureau, a reminder and a token of that journey with the little aunts on which I once embarked unaccompanied by my other self.

It was while I was still enjoying the distinction of having very nearly died that I had another experience in which Grace played no part. We were sitting on the floor one morning, Grace was idly turning the pages of a book and I was in a no less desultory manner perusing *The Springfield Republican* when suddenly I was arrested by a photograph of a middle-aged gentleman on whom I had never laid my eyes. I learned that Andrew J. Wright was dead. He had left a wife and sorrowing children. His life appeared to have been exemplary; he had given generously to charities; his loss would be felt not only by his family but by his native city and the state of Massachusetts. I was profoundly moved and my imagination brushing no doubt the memory of that other gentleman into whose face we had so insolently spat, and overwhelmed by the universal mystery of death and bereavement, I hastily rose, secured a pencil and a piece of paper and began to write in a perfect fervor of inspiration.

Urged by the necessity to express my feelings, without waiting for a word or stopping for a correction, rhymes and meters coming effortlessly into my mind, I brought my poem to a triumphant close. When it was finished I read it from beginning to end.

Andrew J. Wright was a very good man;
I loved him as well as a daughter can.
He loved me as well as a father could,
From a very small child unto womanhood.

One day we were sitting by the sea;
He had in his hand a piece of pie;
He took me upon his bended knee
And told me that soon he was to die.

One very sad and dreary night,
A man by the name of Andrew J. Wright
Lay dying upon his bed;
A girl in her twenties was just in sight
With the coolest of waters bathing his head.
As nights do cease, the clock strikes eleven,
A noble man is now in peace,
For Andrew J. Wright has gone to heaven.

I read it a second time, persuaded that I had written a masterpiece, and showed it to Grace. She read it carefully. "Mary," she said, looking at me with astonishment, "I think it's *wonderful*," and then wistfully, even sorrowfully, she added, "I wish that I had written it."

Fifteen

*W*HEN THE SYRINGA was in bloom and the violets had faded on the bankings and summer had come full tide, there was a change in the climate of our heart and mind from Springfield to New London. We lived in anticipation of all that we expected to experience on our yearly visit to Goshen Point.

Miss Rogers had been very busy getting us ready for departure. It was after midnight; she was sewing in the little room outside our bedroom. Tomorrow we would be leaving for New London. We were about to enter a country where manners and customs differed so greatly from those at home that we were not at all sure whether it was with delight or dread, reluctance or eagerness that we faced tomorrow. Memories of the summers we had spent at Goshen Farm filled our heart. The sewing machine continued to whir. It stopped and started abruptly to whir again. We could tell that Miss Rogers was tired and nervous.

"Miss Rogers, can't you stop your sewing?"

No answer. We pleaded with her again.

"Please, we wish you'd go to bed."

The machine stopped. "What will your aunt think of me if I send you to her in your worn-out clothes? These skirts must be lengthened and the new white dresses finished. I will have plenty of time to rest when you are enjoying yourselves amid the luxuries of your uncle's home."

The sewing machine whirred again. We thought about Miss Rogers and how she would miss us, and as we lay there beside each other exchanging our moods and thoughts as though they derived from a single heart, we moved from the climate of Maple Street into the climate of New London. Familiar phrases wove in and out of our reverie. The great variety of our uncle's costumes, the elegant manner in which he played the role of farmer, came back to us. Our aunt's scrutiny of our clothes and our behavior, Auntie Canfield's disapproval of our presence, induced an uncomfortable sense that our being there placed us in the distressing situation of feeling that we were under great obligations to our relatives for having invited us to stay so long with them. We envisioned the great house with its many rooms, the butler and the subsidiary servants, the French maid, the farm, the gardens, the stables with the many horses and the splendid equipages, our young-lady cousins and their fashionable guests, the magnificence of the meals, and all these items added together emphasizing the fact that we were very poor relations indeed in so fine an establishment.

And yet, and yet tomorrow we would see the ocean; we would go to sleep with the sound of the sea in our ears and in the morning we would wake and go down to breakfast on the pavilion and there before us the meadows and the sea, the smell of honeysuckle, the smell of the daisies and clover, and we would run in the meadows, we would go to the beach and run on the sand.

The whirring of the sewing machine continued lulling us — gulls rose out of the waves and returned again to the sea; sandpipers ran along the track of the waves — tomorrow we would be there; we would take off our shoes and stockings — and so we dropped off into delicious abysses of anticipation and sleep.

The morning of our departure had arrived. The hack that had been ordered from the livery stable to take us to the station was there, and we were sitting in it impatiently waiting for Miss Rogers to get in. She was assisting Patrick Sullivan to get our trunk carefully placed on the box beside the driver.

"Hurry, Miss Rogers, we'll be late."

She climbed into the hack and seated herself. We waved good-bye to Patrick Sullivan. On the way to the station she instructed us as to how we were to behave. She looked sad and very tired. "Remember," she said, "bad conduct on your part is always a mark against me. I want no criticisms from Mrs. Canfield. You must do me credit."

We assured her that we would try our best. She sighed deeply and told us how lonely she would be without us, but that she feared we would forget all about her amid all the pleasures of Goshen Farm. Each of us took hold of a silk-gloved hand and, squeezing it affectionately, we assured her that we couldn't possibly forget her, that we would write her every day. Homesickness vied with our excitement. We wished Miss Rogers were going to the seaside too. It would be terribly hot in Springfield.

At the station there was a great deal of fuss and feather about buying our tickets, checking our trunk, and getting us aboard the train. Finally we were placed in care of the conductor and safely seated. Miss Rogers got out of the train and stood on the platform waiting for it to start. There was a moment of agitation but presently with great heavings and puffings the engine began to move and with many jerkings and backings we were off. We leaned out of the window and as long as we could see an inch of her handkerchief we continued to wave.

Our excitement mounted. In half an hour we would have to change at Palmer. We never felt that we had really started for New London till we were safely seated on the train that awaited us there. Would Miss Rogers have reached home by now, we wondered? She would be hot and tired, she would be thinking of us and very sad.

Now we had stopped at Palmer. There on the other side of the platform was the New London train. We clambered aboard, found a seat upon our favorite side where we could get our first glimpses of the sea. Here on this line — the New London-Northern — no doubt about it, we were on our way to Goshen. The conductor knew us well. He asked us how we were and if we were going to make our summer visit to our aunt and uncle. All of these attentions gave us a great sense of importance.

The day was hot. The red plush seats reeked with the smell of smoke and cinders. The windows were closed against the smoke and soot but when we stopped along the way and the conductor opened the door, a gush of fresh meadow-scented air blew through the car. At Willimantic we were halfway there and from now on the trip would be terribly exciting. Who was likely to be visiting at Goshen? Would we know the visitors? Would we like them? Would they let us go in bathing? Would Aunt Anna have that maid, Marie, whom we disliked so much? Would Mr. Dow be there all summer? We speculated; we wondered. Now at last we came to Norwich, which is on the river Thames. Here there was a sea smell. In only a few minutes we would be arriving. Look! There's our first glimpse of the river. Who would be driving in to meet us? In what kind of carriage would they come? Would it be the big surrey full of visitors and cousins, or the victoria with Aunt Anna and Uncle Jim? Or would they be coming in the *Fidget?* Ah! Here we were. New London! Assisted by the conductor we walked through the train and down the steps. And now we were stepping off onto the platform.

Courage. Here was Uncle Jim approaching. He was dressed in white flannels and on his head, tilted a little to one side, a broad-brimmed Panama. He greeted us rather hurriedly. How much luggage had we got? He hoped it had come along with us. He didn't want to send in the farm wagon another day. It was haying time and they were busy at the farm. We were sure our trunk was put on the train at Palmer, but now we felt a little doubtful. He hurried us to the baggage room to help him identify it and here, to our great relief, it came, trundled in on a long truck from the platform.

"There's our trunk, Uncle Jim."

He gave it a rather critical glance and pointed it out to his farmer, Mr. Emory, who had just come into the baggage room, and he designated two larger, very stylish-looking trunks, which were to be brought out to Goshen Point with ours.

This business dispatched, we accompanied Uncle Jim to the other side of the railroad station where in a great blaze of sunlight there were various waiting carriages, and, among others, a large victoria in which our aunt was comfortably seated beneath her parasol.

"Well, here you are," she said.

"Jump in," commanded our uncle, and obeying him a little awkwardly, for we were afraid of stepping on Aunt

Anna's toes, we got in. We kissed our aunt and at her direction seated ourselves upon the small seat facing her with our backs to the horses. She hoped we had had a pleasant trip. She wondered if Miss Rogers had had the foresight to pack our flannel petticoats — it was usually chilly on the beach.

"Yes, Aunt Anna, we know she did."

We were off and Uncle Jim was seated beside Aunt Anna, crossing his white flannel legs and looking very elegant. What a familiar sound the clip clip clip of the horse's hooves carrying us on our way to Goshen at an ever faster gait. The salt breeze — how exhilarating, how wonderful it smelled. Now we were on the harbor road, the river broadening out to meet the harbor and the sound. Here were the big houses and the Hotel Pequot. And there was our lighthouse.

And did we not remember the foghorn and the donkey braying and the little cart and that gray cottage on the hill where once we lived when we were small? The horses climbed the hill. We passed the cottage. We crossed the bridge at Alewife Cove and then a mile or two beyond — clippity clip, clip, clop.

Now our visit had begun, for this was Goshen Point. On the right were Mr. Chapin's barns and farmhouse. There were his fields and grazing cattle. To the left was our uncle's property — his farm and fields and cattle. And now we were rolling through an avenue of shining willows, tall and shady, and here were the great stone gates through which we passed. And now, oh look — the sea! It rose up before our eyes. Blueness engulfed us. We rounded the driveway with the flower beds in the center shaped like hearts, like anchors, and planted with ageratum, coreopsis, and geraniums. The carriage stopped beneath the porte cochere.

And here coming to greet us were the cousins, Auntie Canfield, Mr. Dow, and the various young ladies. Admonished to be careful and stepping on everybody's toes, we stumbled out of the victoria. There were greetings and kisses and amid all the excitement our aunt commanded us to go immediately to our room — we were tired and must rest before we dressed for supper.

The house was cool and all the windows open to summer and the sea. We were assailed by a sense of arrival that all but overcame us. These rooms, filled with heaven knows how many familiar fragrances from the meadows and the sea, persuaded us achingly that we were really here. Shepherded by Auntie Canfield, we crossed the wide hall and climbed the broad white-oak stairway to the landing halfway up where the tall grandfather's clock ticked loudly. Then on to the large, square upper hall with the family bedrooms off of it and one great window commanding a vast view of sea and sky. We crossed the hall and turned into a narrower, closed stairway leading to the third story and further bedrooms; we climbed these stairs and ran down the hall to our own spacious room. We entered breathless with emotion and rushed to the long window seat confronting the meadows and the sea. We sat down.

"Look, Mary, look!"

"Look, Grace — there's the sea."

We fell into each other's arms and burst into tears.

Sixteen

*W*HEN WE WOKE on the following morning, we ran in our bare feet to the end of the room where from the long seat beneath the row of windows we looked out at the radiant prospect before us. What a perfect summer day! It was exactly as we remembered it — confirmed by the vibrations of every nerve. There was the lightship, there were a trawler and a tugboat and a string of barges. There were no whitecaps today; it would be calm at the beach. Would the tide be low or high when we got there? How could we wait for breakfast to be over? What should we wear when we went down? There were the blue cotton dresses, the brown dresses, and the white ones. Which would Aunt Anna tell us we should not have put on? She'd rather have us wear the dark dresses and our heavy stockings and the high laced boots and our flannel petticoats.

Completely at one in our decision, we got up and began to dress in our plainest and heaviest clothes. They would, we expected, be breakfasting on the pavilion. We must not be late, but we didn't want to be the first to arrive. Dawdling, exchanging the emotions that were filling our heart, we arrayed ourselves in our least attractive costumes and descended to breakfast.

As we passed from the hall onto the large piazza, familiarly known as the pavilion, we seemed to step into a vast acreage of blue air and sky and sea. And what a blast of fragrance, honeysuckle, pollens delicately blended, a breeze from off the sea and from the meadows, the morning song of birds. Breakfast was in full swing; our aunt, all dressed in white, was pouring coffee behind a great array of cups and saucers. The scene looked extremely gala — flowers, summer dresses, flowered china, finger bowls, cantaloupes, and clean white damask.

"Good morning," said Aunt Anna. "You are late."

We kissed her and took the places chosen for us, Grace beside our Cousin Anna, while I sat next to Rebecca. Both girls had on the loveliest of dresses, one in lavender, the other all in pink. Auntie Canfield was beside me and gave us both a disapproving glance. Chapin was on Aunt Anna's right, and next to him his tutor, Mr. Dow, who bestowed upon us both a covert wink. One of the young ladies whose trunk had come out with us was already seated. She was a perfect beauty with large blue eyes and golden hair — Miss Mamie Williams. The other visitor, a Miss Nina le Boussilour, was just arriving. She made a great many apologies. And now everyone was here but Uncle Jim.

He was coming. We could smell him coming. His cologne blotted out the honeysuckle. He was dressed in white — white coat and trousers and his brown shoes shining like mahogany and a blue tie and a blue cornflower in his buttonhole.

"Good morning, Mamá," he said, chipper as a lark. And then he kissed both his daughters and saluted the two young ladies. Sitting down he said, "And who have we here in our midst this morning?" — referring, of course, to us. He asked whose chicken coop we planned to rob.

"The twins," said our aunt, "are going to the beach this morning." Everyone assembled, breakfast progressed. There was much planning for the day. A trip on the *Fidget* and lunch at Fishers Island or Watch Hill was suggested. Aunt Anna declared there was not time to plan for such an outing. Cousin Rebecca said, "Oh no, Papá." At which our uncle gave her a quick suspicious look. Cousin Anna said, "Oh yes, Papá." There was discussion for and against. We caught a breeze of disapproval directed toward our oldest cousin. We thought we knew the meaning of all this.

But would breakfast never end? We'd had enough of all the talk and all the people. We needed to get away, to run, to feel the joy of freedom — to stay an instant longer was more than we could bear. Finally, getting up courage, we said, "May we be excused, Aunt Anna?" She asked us to come to her to be inspected. "Have you got on your flannel petticoats?" she asked, and lifted our skirts. "But those stockings — are these proper stockings for the beach?"

"They're what we thought you wanted us to wear, Aunt Anna."

She let us go.

Released! Completely off the human tether we ran straight into the bright acres of earth and sky and sea. We appeared to have no objective; our need was to run to release our happiness, which was made the more intense because there lurked beneath it an awareness of human affairs that bore no relationship to this condition of pure joy. Where should we go? Our intention had been to go to the beach, but we would stay here and become a part of this bright meadow. We could not fly or sing like birds, but we could join the dance of summer. Come, let us take hands, let us run across the meadow. Listen, the meadowlarks are singing as they rise. A bobolink swings on a stalk of timothy, bending it over backwards with his song. Grasshoppers spring out of the high grass, making a clack and clatter as they open up their fanlike wings; they fly into our face; they stain our petticoats with spittle.

Butterflies hover, spread their luminous wings and descend upon the buttercups and the daisies. Let us join the dance of summer!

Seventeen

THE SEA LOOKED immense, the horizon far off and sharply divided from the air and the sky. The tide was low just as we said it would be. And everything was exactly the same as it had been last year. There was a big dock running out into the water and the bathhouses stood on either side of the dock. The sand was just as white as always and there was that long stretch of hard wet beach with the flecks of foam and the tracks of the waves still marked on the sand. What an invigorating smell! How exciting it was to sniff it again.

What should we do? Should we be lazy awhile and lie in the heat, on the blazing sand? Or should we run as fast as we possibly could? Those rocks at the end of the Chapins' property would all be uncovered; we could look for rock crabs and lift up the big stones and try to catch the crabs before they scuttled away. But we'd have to take off our stockings and shoes. And did Aunt Anna say that we could do so?

— Well, she didn't say we couldn't. Off we ran over the long stretch of beach until we reached our destination. Here we took off our shoes and our stockings and, leaving them behind us, stepped out among the rocks and the stones and the deep and the shallower pools. The water felt delicious lapping our feet. But be careful, the rocks are slippery and the barnacles sharp.

What a beautiful pool. We bent over it. The water was translucent and clear. The pool was paved with white sand delicately scalloped as though a thousand little wavelets had slipped in without a sound to make a tiny beach. A small green crab shuttled across the sand. He lifted a neat green claw. Above him an immaculate minnow was suspended. Then descending suddenly, he wiggled his silver belly in the sand, disturbing, sullying the water. We waited and watched the water clear. There was the crab and there was the minnow swimming and on the sand a mussel shell shone brightly and the snail shells appeared to move a little as we watched.

When we had had our fill of all these minute wonders, we sighed in grave appreciation and removing our shadows from the water, proceeded to step out again among the slippery rocks, rolling a big stone over or lifting up a shelf of shallow rock to see what we would find. Seaweed, clusters of mussels, bunches of snails, and thousands of barnacles clinging to them. Sometimes, but not always, a green crab sidled off as fast as possible. So we continued making toward the channel between the two large rocks on which we intended to lie. Here the sea came in with a great roaring noise, lifting the seaweeds from the rocks, spreading them out, floating them off in delicate filaments of the loveliest hues and colors — pink and brown and lettuce-green and purple — swaying them out; and then when

the waters retreated, slapping them up against the rocks again
— a formless indiscriminate mass of brown. Stretched each on
her rock, we lay entranced with the sound of the gurgling,
roaring waters — the movement, the changing forms and colors.

But suddenly lost to time and obedience, with one accord
we rose and looked about us. What time was it getting to be?
It must be late. Was that the *Fidget* steaming out from the
New London harbor? No, too large for her, but there were a
big white schooner and two sailboats and a string of barges,
and out along the far horizon there was a long, black streak
of smoke. They would be coming down to bathe. But we
couldn't go in. We could not bathe until July the Fourth — an
adamant rule. Well, we could watch the others and, forgetting
our shoes and stockings, we raced each other to the dock and
there we lay down flat on our stomachs in the hot sand and
began to play the game that we always played when we were
here — mining precious stones, for this clean white sand was
full of tiny gems, blue and red and green and amethyst and
topaz. We picked them up with considerable difficulty and
laid them out on our palms for inspection.

"Here's a ruby, Mary."

"Oh look, I have an enormous sapphire."

"Here's an amethyst and here's a topaz."

The waves murmured at our backs. They broke, retreated, and
broke again. The sun was hot — it set the air to swimming,
wavering before our eyes, and it was all so lazy-lovely — conversing as we mined our tiny jewels —

"Auntie Canfield hates him . . ."

"Yes, did you see the way she looked at him at breakfast?"

"Didn't I!"

"And why does Cousin Rebecca say she doesn't want to go off on the *Fidget?* I should think she'd try to fool them and pretend she did."

". . . Look, what a clear white diamond."

But they had come, the bathers with their towels across their arms. First the family from the other house. Mr. Lindley Chapin, such a very decorative gentleman with his wonderful dark beard and the turquoise rings upon his fingers and such a high-pitched voice and almost always laughing. And there were the two little girls, Katherine and Cornelia, dressed in pretty ruffled frocks. And the young boy, Paul. And there was Marguerite, older than we by several years and oh so very handsome with her long dark curls and her perfectly beautiful dresses. We'd rather be Marguerite Chapin than anybody on the earth. She had a donkey and a donkey cart. We greeted each other and Mr. Chapin made one of his funny frivolous remarks. Mrs. Chapin, his second wife, was not the mother of Marguerite. She was coming down with Uncle Jim, who had his towel and some clean linen in a large bright-colored basket; the others would be following.

But heavens, there was Marie, Aunt Anna's maid. She'd come down to fetch us and was in an awful stew. She scolded in French and it was hard to understand what she was saying. She couldn't understand us. But we gathered that she was telling us that our Aunt Anna wanted us at the house at once, for we must change our dresses. She saw we had no shoes and stockings. She continued to scold.

"Yes, yes, we'll go and get them . . ."

And we ran, we positively tore to the place where we had discarded them, and we put them on; following Marie's injunctions, we walked slowly and apprehensively up to the house.

Eighteen

On sundays at Goshen everyone descended dressed in their cleanest and gayest summer costumes. After breakfast on the pavilion we were immediately subjected to strict Sabbatarian rules and regulations. We must attend with the rest of the family the services that were solemnly conducted in the parlor, where, seated on a chintz-covered sofa, we endured the weekly ordeal with singular propriety.

Never had four walls more graciously enclosed the very essence of a midsummer day; the fresh breeze blown in over the honeysuckle vines laden with salt air and the fragrance of the meadows moved gently, very gently about us. And to add to this sense of summer — distributing, fairly chucking it around the room, a medley of the most harmonious hues and colors, pinks and pale blues and delicate lavenders — sweet-peas in a Dresden china bowl on the piano and more of these in a Dresden basket on an adjacent stand; on the mantel two rosy cupids upholding candelabra fairly sprouting forget-me-nots and roses, and as though to spread all this pinkness, blueness, an Aubusson carpet displayed further cupids, ribbons, and hydrangeas. Aunt Anna was the very embodiment of Unitarian piety, and this she endeavored, not without a modicum of success, to impose upon both of us. It was only necessary to sit beside her to be made aware, by the expression on her countenance and the manner in which she encased her body as well as her soul in her unshatterable faith, of the variety of her religious moods and consolations.

Uncle Jim conducted the services and at a signal from him the assembled company rose, bowed, repeated the Lord's Prayer and sat down while he read us a chapter from one of the Gospels. Then Cousin Rebecca went to the piano, whereupon we rose again and sang to her accompaniment a familiar hymn.

It was with inexpressible relief that, throwing off our churchly mood, we all assembled on the pavilion where we immediately put ourselves into the hands of our genial uncle, now fully prepared to conduct us through another Sunday ritual — the weekly inspection of his beloved farm. Dressed as usual in white and with a flower — a bachelor's button or a red rose — in his buttonhole, he shepherded his gay procession, flourishing his cane as he marched at our head to point out various landmarks on his property. Over the lawn we went, past the greenhouses and the garden, past the stable with the brightly colored windmill turning noisily in the breeze, on into a shaded avenue of willows, and then to a sunny stretch of road between privet hedges. On the right, fields of waving corn and on the left, with the blue sea beyond, a field with grazing cattle, some marshes, and a creek.

We crossed the creek on a rustic bridge. Here the two of us lingered behind. It was always a delight to look over the railing and watch the current when the tide was high and look for crabs that cling to the seaweed swirling around the piers. We ran from one side of the bridge to the other.

"Oh look at this one, he's a monster."

"There are two on my side, green and blue."

We lagged far behind. The others called to us; only by running over the last hot stretch of road could we catch up with the procession by the time they reached the farm — "Little Goshen." The barns were all red and down below them was the farmyard with the henhouses and the chicken coops. There was a corncrib and the icehouse; there was the little dairy and the red farmhouse, the first place we always visited. It had been in this house that Mrs. Emory told us of our parents' death, and we never saw her without experiencing a vague recollection of sorrow. She was slamming the screen door and was coming out to greet us. She invited us in and we all filed into the front parlor. Such a stuffy room, smelling the way farmhouses do with all the windows shut against the sun and air. Everyone who could find a chair sat down. The conversation was about the weather and how we all were and what a fine year for haying. There was a cottage organ and on the wall in a large gilt frame was an enormous photograph of our uncle in his great sable coat. He himself was in the office talking to Mr. Emory about his cattle and the crops and the expense of running his farm.

When he returned with Mr. Emory, he hastened us all out to continue our tour of inspection. It was good to be in the sun again. The next place we visited was the dairy — a little red house in the middle of a duck pond with a bridge over half the pond which we must take to reach it. We went over one by one. When we entered, how cool, how pleasant it was with the shining pans of milk set out on shelves along the walls and the churn and the icebox full of lovely pats of butter. After the dairy we headed for the barnyard. The sun streamed down upon us. It was hot as hot. There were a lot of hens running around and one big hen with a string of fluffy yellow chicks following her. Old Shep, the farm dog, lay in the sun biting his fleas. One solitary peacock, rather ragged and forlorn, emitted a raucous scream. We stopped at the pigpens — phui, what a smell. How do they get to be such filthy creatures? There was a great sow exposing her fat stomach with a row of newborn piglets tugging at her teats, the prettiest things we ever saw with ears as pink as seashells and those funny flat pink snouts and all as clean as they could be. We lagged behind to watch them.

"Come on now," they were calling. They were going to the cow barn. This was Uncle Jim's favorite place — no wonder, such a barn! Clean as a whistle with white sand strewn over the floor and fresh straw in all the stalls, and over the stalls the names of the cows in bright enamel letters: "Goshen Belle," "Queen of Goshen," and all the rest. There was a prize bull, "The Bull of Bashan." Oh look, a newborn calf. How sweet she was — a little Jersey lying over on her skinny haunches and looking up at us with her beautiful bulging sorrowful brown eyes. "What are you going to name her, Uncle Jim?"

He waited a minute or two. Well, he didn't know.

"How about 'Empress of Goshen'?" He chuckled, and we followed him out of the cowbarn and went from there to the hay barn. Here the lofts were crammed to the rafters with hay smelling warm and sweet brought in from the fields and meadows. There were the big farm implements and the mowing machine and the big horse rake for piling up the hay behind it.

The tour was over and we were out in the blazing sun again and on our way to the beach. The Sunday mood possessed us, for that day everything was strictly scheduled. Quite a business at the beach when our gala procession arrived for bathing and the family from the other house, all got up for Sunday too, added to our sense that special manners and behavior were imposed on us today. We could bathe, but we must remember that this was Sunday and we mustn't have too good a time. Our clothes must not be mussed, for we would have to keep them in condition for the midday dinner, which would require a very special cleanliness and decorum. After the long hot walk, the plunge into the cool salt water — we couldn't stay in as long as usual, and we were reminded frequently that romping and boisterous behavior must be ruled out today. Doing our best to conform to these arbitrary rules we managed to bathe and dress ourselves and proceed up to the house before the rest of the family had emerged from the bathhouses.

Running on ahead of the others, ravenous and thinking of the great Sunday feast awaiting us, we approached the large house that always seemed to us so enormously impressive. There it stood capriciously shingled and clapboarded and painted in various shades of red and green with its astonishing architectural caprices and inventions — its pavilion, its pinnacles, its balconies and verandas — a cross between the Kremlin and a cuckoo clock. What would Miss Rogers think if she could see it? We ran up the steps, crossed the pavilion and entered the house. We must get to our room as quickly as possible because we didn't want Auntie Canfield to pounce upon us to tell us what we must do to make ourselves presentable. Arriving unobserved, we brushed our hair, washed the salt water from our faces, and sat down upon the window seat to watch the bathers coming from the beach. We would not descend until we heard the gong that summoned us for dinner.

As we sat down, separated but as always opposite each other, we were as much delighted by the grace and beauty of the table and its appointments as we were discomfited by the presence of so much pomp and ceremony. How sumptuous, how glittering, how lavish a display. The large white damask tablecloth, and every napkin folded like a lily with a crusty roll inside; the beautiful, the best, the Sunday china, the shining goblets and wineglasses, the shining silver and, in the center of the table, that great bowl of fruit, peaches and pears, grapes and nectarines, so beautifully arranged that who would dare to take a single fruit for fear of destroying the wondrous pyramid. Then there were the silver dishes filled with candies — peppermints, delectable chocolates. We would have our eyes upon those chocolates throughout the meal, choosing the one we wished to take when they were passed around. The long meal would have its moments of oppressiveness and moments fraught with interest, curiosity and signals stealthily exchanged. A large part of the conversation was sure to be given over to discussion about who should use the horses. There were so many in the stable, but some were lame and others should be exercised and which horses should be used for what was a matter for endless discussion.

Today Aunt Anna said peremptorily, "In any case, even if one of the roans has gone a little lame, I want them both this afternoon."

"Very well, my dear Mamá," answered our uncle, who seemed to have all these equestrian problems in his hands. "You shall have them." Then Cousin Rebecca put in a plea for the dogcart and a small chestnut called Melissa. The suggestion was looked upon with great disapproval. Uncle Jim said emphatically, "NO!" And Auntie Canfield muttered under her breath, "I never seen such works!" Aunt Anna turned to Mr. Dow. She hoped his afternoon was free because she wanted him to drive with her to discuss plans for the coming winter. Alive to all the implications this discussion entailed, we exchanged silent conjecture.

After the stupendous feast was over, coffee and liqueurs were served on the pavilion. Uncle Jim smoked his cigar. Everyone seemed languid, drowsy. The talk moved from one familiar topic to another and seemed very dull and uninspired. Presently, we went and lay down together in one of the comfortable hammocks.

Time pivoted around the landmarks of our visit. Contented with our unity of mood, the perfect chime and sequence of our thoughts, we passed mostly in silence from one topic to another.

"Will Cousin Rebecca marry Chapin's tutor?"

"You know what Auntie Canfield said?"

"Rebecca Rumrill wants to marry her father's hired man."

We swung, lazily enjoying the movement of the hammock, exchanging queries and calculations.

"How many weeks since our arrival?"

"How many weeks before we leave?"

"Miss Rogers must be missing us. We've only written once."

There was a drone of conversation. "Would you say that we'd be glad to leave or sorry?" Down on the beach the waves were breaking. The talk was interrupted. There was laughter. Someone snored.

"Maybe we'd say that we'd be glad."

"And maybe not."

The waves continued breaking. The fresh wind blew across our faces. We nodded; we closed our eyes. We fell asleep.

Nineteen

$\mathcal{I}$T WAS AUNT ANNA'S afternoon at home. We
had experienced many of these gala Thursdays with guests arriving in their line carriages, ladies and gentlemen disporting
themselves on the lawns or on the pavilion — gentlemen in
white trousers and colorful neckties and hatbands, ladies in
long ruffled dresses, carrying parasols or wearing large flowery
hats. We knew many of them by name and those we did not
know we endowed with names of our own invention. Always
possessed of a mad desire to imitate, we usually controlled our
need for hilarity and behaved on the whole pretty well.

We were deeply attracted by the grace and the color, the
laughter and ease and elegance — the beauty of it all. Knowing
that we were not there as actual members of these bright occasions and suffering from a feeling of exclusion, we were
seldom without a vague sense of heartache and yearning.

Today we were dressed and ready to go down but we had not yet got up the courage to do so. We'd heard the carriages on the gravel arriving and departing. There would be a big crowd, for the day was so beautiful. Aunt Anna had given us our orders, "You must make your 'appearance' this afternoon." Apprehensively we smoothed out our spotless muslins. We looked at each other, each trying to appraise her own appearance — the broad blue sash, the curls, the lovely ruffled dress, the smile, the expression, all seemed in order. But we felt disinclined to leave the sanctity of our own room. We could hear the voices and the laughter; it was getting late; there must be a big crowd down there already. Here comes another carriage.

Come. Should we go down? The hall was emptied of all sounds and servants. We took hold of hands and descended; first our own narrow stairway, then into the upper hall; we crossed the hall and peeked over the balustrade, listening; voices, laughter ascended.

In the lower hall and opposite the door onto the pavilion, we waited. Deciding upon a new strategy, we ran through the hall to the front door; we listened. No carriage was approaching. We dashed out, crossed under the porte cochere and onto the lawn.

Nobody on the lawn. Should we steal away and go to the beach? We might go to the summerhouse and see if we could catch Ruby and Emerald. They were pretty sure at this hour to come to the honeysuckle on the dunes. Listen! There was another carriage. We ran over the lawn, now in full sight of the pavilion. If Aunt Anna should see us, she'd call us to come and make our "appearance."

The beauty of the scene, the summer afternoon, the cloudless sky, the blue sea overcame us. There toward the west where the sea entered the creek that went on flowing through our uncle's marshes, the bar of white white sand and at the mouth of the creek gulls ascending and descending. Beneath our feet the lawn was freshly cut and smelled delicious. And there was the sweeter smell of new-mown hay — great swaths of it spread out to dry upon the meadow with the bobolinks and meadowlarks hovering over, singing their summer tunes. Our sharp delight in all this radiance was mixed with other feelings, scarcely explored as yet, but moving into mysterious realms: a sense of pain, a longing for — who knows what? Something closely allied perhaps to this large ache that seemed to fill the heart. We would like more than anything to simply run away, to go racing, flying over the meadows, forgetting everything but our delight in the lovely moment.

But we were restrained from doing so — we knew the meadow was not ours to appropriate, it belonged this afternoon to Uncle Jim, who would at any minute now make his appearance on the enchanted scene.

"Grace and Mary, I want you to come." There was nothing for it but to obey. We crossed the lawn, mounted the steps to the pavilion. How many people, such a chime of voices — so much laughter. Aunt Anna beckoned us. She was talking to a tall lady in a pink dress who carried a closed parasol over her right arm, very elegant indeed.

"This," said Aunt Anna, "is Mrs. Williams."

She smiled and said she used to know our mother and our father, and this deposited in our heart a number of feelings difficult to explain but making us somehow feel less alien. After this she made the usual remarks — how exactly alike we were, and which was Grace and which was Mary; then she kissed us and we were dismissed.

Refreshments were appearing. Tinkling pitchers full of lemonade and grape juice, cakes and delicious cookies, small sandwiches. These were set on iron tables with a quantity of shining glasses. Aunt Anna did not ask us to assist, so when we were offered our choice, lemonade or grape juice, a little abashed at our own temerity, we chose the latter and rather hesitantly took it from the tray, helped ourselves to cake, and were about to carry our refreshments to a table on the lawn when we were joined by Mr. Dow.

We were delighted to see him. Now that we knew he wanted to marry our favorite cousin, he had become the most romantic of figures. But what attached him to us more than anything else was that he felt very much as we did about these afternoons, indeed about a great deal that went on at Goshen. He never felt that he was a member of any bright occasion. He enjoyed our burlesque and buffoonery. He was surprised that we had kept so clean and proper and wondered how we were managing to bear up.

"Oh look, Mary! Look, Mr. Dow — there's Uncle Jim."

And there he was to be sure, riding the great hay rake from the farm, gathering up the swaths of hay, pressing the lever with his small mahogany foot, depositing first one mound of hay, making a skillful turn, depositing another mound, and all with so much style you could hardly believe your eyes — as though those great farm horses were winners of blue ribbons and he was driving them through a fine park, his shoulders high, his white flannel suit shining in the sun and his broad Panama hat, trimmed with a striking red scarf, a bit aslant on his beautiful white head. All the guests had seen him. They rushed to the front of the pavilion and stood in admiration at his exploit.

"How Mr. Rumrill loves his farm!" "A genuine farmer." The exclamations passed from mouth to mouth while Uncle Jim continued with his raking.

"Whoa, Joan. Whoa, Jean." Making the skillful turns, pressing down the mahogany foot, the blue sea behind him, the sky enfolding him. The sea gulls dipping and the white sails shining on the water — the very core and center of that radiant scene. The three of us enjoyed the spectacle together.

Uncle Jim came up from the hayfield mopping his brow with his big silk handkerchief, smiling, accepting congratulations. We said good-bye to Mrs. Williams. Our aunt dismissed us and we were free at last.

The carriages drove away, the laughter and the voices faded. The ladies in their lovely dresses and parasols, the gentlemen in their beautiful trousers and colored hat bands vanished. The bright pageant was carried off and away to await another Thursday afternoon.

Twenty

$\mathcal{I}$T WAS LATE. We would depart tomorrow morning. The candles were blown out. We were there on the window seat, thinking of our departure in the morning. There's the Montauk light; it's flashing white and red. There was the steamer. It saluted the lighthouse as it passed. Tomorrow night we would be in Springfield. The dresses we would wear were hanging in the closet and clean underclothes were neatly laid out on a chair just in case of wreck or accident on the train.

We had had a pleasant visit. On the whole we'd been quite good. This afternoon we had taken a drive with Aunt Anna. She took us to say good-bye to Mrs. Emory and the farm, then we drove away outside of Goshen, into town by the back road and home the usual way, passing the *Pequot* and the lighthouse and our old cottage on the hill. Every sight was memory — all the arrivals and departures, all the visits — and knowing we'd not see Goshen for another year. We let her do the talking mostly. We had, she said, but with few exceptions, been very good indeed upon this visit. She had written to tell this to Miss Rogers.

Sitting there together on the last night of our visit, in and out of all the memories, we were intimately joined in living through those two misdemeanors to which she had referred. We knew that they would be among those little dramas of the heart that time would neither alter nor erase.

That day they had the bathing party and we dropped the shoehook out of the window and it got stuck on the roof below and we didn't dare crawl out to get it. Remember how we shied a hairbrush at it just to knock it down and how the hairbrush reached the lawn and not the shoehook? We went a little crazy and began to shy anything that we could find to hit it — toothbrushes, shoes and combs and pairs of drawers and pairs of stockings, our red hot-water bag, the tooth mug, most everything we threw down reached the lawn but didn't hit the shoehook. And then the voices, laughter, and the people coming up from bathing and Uncle Jim ahead dressed in white and carrying his basket and wearing the Panama with the bright scarf he wore to rake the meadow.

The way he stopped short when he saw all those shocking objects strewn about the lawn and glanced up at our window and, forgetting all about his party, rushed into the house; and we, hearing the door slam, waiting together, hearing his voice commanding us to come directly down into his den.

It wasn't so much the being spanked as it was that Uncle Jim had done it. If it had been Auntie Canfield or even Aunt Anna — but Uncle Jim! His anger — unbuttoning our drawers and laying the bottoms bare and he, dressed up so finely and smelling so strongly of his cologne, and each one having that spanking double, standing there to see the other get it. Not so much the pain of those angry little smacks, it was the shame we felt about it — wishing *he* hadn't done it.

"Yes, Aunt Anna," "No, Aunt Anna," we replied in answer to her inquiries about our schooling and our health and the condition of our summer clothes — passing the harbor, whiffing a long breath of the sea. And all the while remembering the day Ruby and Emerald came when we least expected them and hovered above the honeysuckle among the wild grapevines and the beach plums and the bay leaves on the dunes beside the summerhouse. We'd seen them so often and in other summers thinking how impossible — how great a wonder it would be to catch one of them in our own bare hands. And there they were — that sheen, all green and bronze on Emerald's neck and shoulders with his beak inserted in the honeysuckle's throat; not a part of him that touched the little flower — floating upon the air, quivering, drinking his drop of honey. And there on a nearby vine was Ruby with a red jewel beneath her throat and her breast so soft, so yellow-white, sipping honey from another flower. Everything — the air, the flowers, the two bright birds afloat, aquiver. Then Ruby flew away and made a lashing with her wings. Up into the air, way up so you could hardly see her and down again circling, lashing. Then Emerald flew off and you could hear him flying — up, up into the air. In an instant Ruby was back with her beak in the honeysuckle's throat.

"Quick, there's Ruby, quick."

And wonder of perfect wonders, we'd captured Ruby, cupped our hands around her beating wings, had her closed up tight, tight — our prisoner.

"Run. Don't drop her."

And here we were together with her, running. We would take her to our room; we'd close the windows on her. We would keep her. She would be ours together —

We ran up the steps, crossed the pavilion, brought her into the house and just inside the door — she got free, swooping about the hall so wildly, and in a minute the hall was full of people giving directions, shouting orders. The butler chasing her with a white cloth and the parlor maid making at her with a feather duster. Aunt Anna was giving orders and Auntie Canfield snooping around — and though they didn't scold, just acted as though we were guilty, responsible for the disaster, they made us feel so awful. The thing that seemed so strange, so difficult to understand, was that not one among them guessed even for a minute, how impossible a thing it was — a perfect wonder — to catch a hummingbird in our bare hands. Just standing round and acting as though we'd brought an eagle or a vulture or some big bird they'd never seen into the house instead of Ruby.

Do you suppose Aunt Anna told Miss Rogers about Ruby and about the day we got spanked? Well, if she did, Miss Rogers wouldn't think we'd been so awful. We ruminated, looking out across the meadow to the sea.

There was the light again — now red, now white. What a clear night. We could hear the waves — only just a murmur. And the crickets chirping in the meadow — on the whole it had been a lovely summer.

Twenty-one

*M*ISS ROGERS WAS at the station to meet us. We saw her before she saw us. She had stopped the conductor and was questioning him excitedly. She was wearing what appeared to be the wings of a dove and a blue bow set at a crazy angle on the back of her head. The first glimpse of her pale face thus exposed to our attention gave her back to us in all her freakish variety and offered us time to adjust our mood to the joyousness required by the moment. As soon as she saw us she made a somewhat flustered gesture and flew hurriedly in our direction. We rushed into her arms.

After the usual difficulties about our bag and baggage had been solved, we finally found ourselves headed for home.

There was always a stiffness about her when we first came home, as though she were suspicious that so much elegance and luxury had inclined us against her and our life at Maple Street.

We bombarded her with questions.

"Did Rebecca and the boys get off this morning for Goshen?"

"How's Patrick Sullivan?"

"Did you miss us very much? Won't it be nice being alone — just the three of us?"

We walked one on either side of her, rather oppressed by the heat after the cool breezes of Goshen but increasingly glad to be back. There was something pleasant about it, all the familiar houses coming into view with the shuttered, midsummer look and everything going along at a lazy hot-weather pace, something nostalgic, recalling other returns.

Miss Rogers asked sarcastically, "Does Mrs. Canfield still display herself in jet beads and taffeta? Does she still deliver her opinions with her usual eloquence?"

After assuring her that Auntie Canfield was just the same as ever, we went on with our own eager questions — was the fruit ripe on the bankings? Had Patrick made a new asparagus bed? Had she persuaded him to take another pledge?

Seeing her stiffness beginning to abate, we offered further information. "Auntie Canfield told Mr. Chapin that Cousin Rebecca is going to marry her father's hired man."

Miss Rogers emitted several artificial guffaws. "Whatever opinion Mrs. Rumrill's *housekeeper* holds of Mr. Dow will, I am sure, decide the entire issue."

In response to the really important question, had Aunt Anna written her about Emerald and Ruby and the spanking we got from Uncle Jim, Miss Rogers replied that she had had a long letter reporting that our behavior had been reasonably good. And then completely thawed out, the old intimacy fully restored, she confided, "I have some secrets — oh, very interesting — but I will tell you later."

"Why can't you tell us now?"

"All in good time, my darlings."

"Are you going to get married?"

"No," she said taking the question seriously. "It isn't that."

"Well then what is it? Is it about Rebecca? Philip? James? Not Patrick Sullivan?"

"No," she said emphatically, putting an end to the teasing.

At this moment we came into full view of our own house. We ran on ahead past the great elm trees and across the lawn, up the walk and into the house ahead of Miss Rogers. Back again — home.

The house was cool and dim and shrouded and gave out many welcoming summer smells that were subtly mingled with all we had felt on other returns from Goshen. In the south parlor the shutters were closed and the light came through and lay in waving bands upon the floor. Miss Rogers joined us and was happy in our delight at being back again.

"Does everything look as usual?" she inquired.

"Oh yes," we said, embracing her.

Observing suddenly a big empty space on the wall above the sofa and a great square where the paper was clean and the pattern distinct, we asked in some dismay, "But where is Aunt Anna's painting?"

Miss Rogers looked pained.

"What happened? Where is Aunt Anna's picture?" we insisted.

Various objects in the house had been selected by our grandmother to go to certain members of the Rumrill family; these were always referred to as belonging not to us but to whomever they had been willed.

"Patrick stepped in it," she said reluctantly.

"Stepped in it? How could he step in a picture hanging on the wall?"

"I had had it taken down. It needed oiling — you know how careful I always am of your aunt's possessions — "

"Well, then what happened?"

". . . When I had it face down on the parlor floor . . ."

"Was he drunk, Miss Rogers?"

Forced to reply she said apologetically, "He thought it was a piece of brown paper.

Doubled over with mirth and chanting in imitation of Patrick, "Ah Miss Ratchers, I thot it was a paice of brown paiper," we lifted our feet and planted them heavily on the floor.

"I am having it repaired at my own expense."

Actually distressed by the absence of a familiar object, we asked Miss Rogers when it would come back, and receiving no reply we ran off to greet the other rooms awaiting our inspection. The house seemed strangely empty without Rebecca and the boys.

At suppertime we were aware how lovingly Miss Rogers had planned for our return. She had gone to the garden to pick whatever roses there were for the center of the table. She had put out the best china too, and made everything as gay and pretty as possible. We had peaches and cream for dessert and a beautiful sponge cake that she had made herself. At Goshen they would be having supper out on the pavilion, there would be the fresh breeze from the sea, the sound of the waves, the smell of the honeysuckle and night approaching. But this, we told ourselves, was much nicer. It was hot and there was no sea breeze, but how lovely to be here chatting and growing more and more accustomed to being back in our beloved house.

There was a great deal to talk about. There had been no further mention of the secrets that we could hardly wait to have her divulge. Finally in one breath we exclaimed, "Now tell us about the secrets."

She insisted that the proper time had not yet arrived.

"But why can't you tell us now?"

"Your aunt wrote that I had better wait until you have been at home a few days."

"But that isn't saying you *can't*. You won't be disobeying orders — it's not as though you're going to break a promise."

Our logic seemed persuasive. She gave in. It was plain to see she was dying to tell us. She started off rather secretively lowering her voice, a little coy about it all.

"Mr. Louis Dow," she said, "your cousin Chapin's tutor, is coming here to stay with us at Maple Street when the family returns to Springfield."

The surprise was overwhelming. "Mr. Dow coming to live with us? Where is he going to sleep?"

"In the little sewing room adjacent to your bedroom. I will take the sewing machine into my room. Moreover," she continued, enlarging the surprise, "he is going to start preparing James and Philip, as well as your cousin Chapin, for college."

"Will they have the lessons here?"

"No, at Chestnut Street. He will make this house his home," she replied, laying special emphasis on *this* house.

"But why must this house be his home?" Through hints and innuendoes and a series of revealing expressions that flitted across her face, we knew she was aware of the real reason Mr. Dow was not wanted at Chestnut Street. She was pretty sarcastic about it all: "It's the almighty dollar your aunt and uncle appreciate. Mr. Dow can only offer culture and education."

"And that's the reason they don't want him to marry Cousin Rebecca?"

Miss Rogers put her handkerchief to her face and laughed hilariously. "Your aunt *says* she is sending him to us because of the excellent effect he has upon your brothers."

"What's the other secret, Miss Rogers? You've only told us one."

She was loath to be cut off from conversing further about Mr. Dow. Looking at us gravely she changed her manner and her mood. "Your aunt questions my ability to go on with your education. She says it is high time for you to go to school."

Uncertain whether to be pleased by this information, we inquired eagerly, "Where, Miss Rogers? Miss Kimball's?"

"Where else? I presume Miss Kimball has persuaded your aunt that it is time you had more social as well as educational advantages than you could possibly receive from me.

We could see that it hurt her to continue with the subject and, more ready to digest the information than to assure her of her ability, we fell into silence.

When we were finally lying side by side in bed we listened to the incessant music of the night, the song of the katydids swinging from branch to branch, from bough to bough and on and on into the surrounding darkness. They seemed to say, "Home again, home again," as though the thousand choirs sang in unison.

Remember the beach and the meadow and the farm — remember the pavilion and the honeysuckle; remember Ruby; remember Emerald and on and on from branch to branch from bough to bough; summer's over and the winter's coming; we will go to school and Mr. Dow will live with us. Amid this clamor in the trees and the clamor of memories and expectations, a single thought is passed back and forth between us, comforting and substantial: we are back at Maple Street — "Home again, home again."

Twenty-two

A SUNNY ROOM, the light streaming through all the windows, the flick and flash of goldfish in a crystal bowl, pots of geraniums along the window sill, girls in pigtails and plaid dresses, boys in serge coats with Windsor ties and collars, and our teacher on her platform doing her best to keep the children under control — this was Miss Kimball's classroom.

Two pairs of eyes, four ears operating as though upon a single mind, informed us — we were acutely aware of all the other children; they pointed at us, they snickered, they hid their giggles behind their hands, they regarded us as freaks. This knowledge was so stimulating that it suggested untried powers and resources. At first we drew upon these cautiously, getting our bearings, testing our audience. Then, as we grew more confident we began to draw upon them perilously — perilously.

There was a boy called Sam who prior to our arrival had been the school's most difficult problem and who did his best to hold his reputation by vying with us in every way he could. But what chance had Sam when he had but a single brain and each of us was armed with all the ingenuity of two? We changed our seats, causing Miss Kimball to invite Grace to recite Mary's lesson or Mary to recite Grace's. Then, arising in a state of wild excitement, each divulging the mistake, we grew delirious with mirth. We laughed, we shouted, we chucked our nonsense words, "Hack of the Karoussi," "Monkey Black Bat," around the room — which was Mary? which was Grace? — Miss Kimball didn't know, the children didn't know, and by that time neither did we. Pandemonium reigned. We were possessed by a single demon, in the grip of something beyond our control — the strain of being two identities instead of one.

Almost every day some devilish idea presented itself. We devised schemes meant not only to entertain the children but to confound the teacher. Our success emboldened us and mischief spread contagiously. The strain upon her and the disorder in the classroom rocked the school. She was at her wits' end. She consulted our guardians, she talked with Miss Rogers; our withdrawal was imminent. But more serious still was the defeat of Miss Kimball herself. She had lost heart; she felt she could teach no longer.

When we found ourselves at home again, we had not only to bear the chagrin of being dismissed but the shame of having all but wrecked Miss Kimball's school.

What a relief to be all day at Maple Street again! To be sure, we were under something of a cloud, but Miss Rogers, although she pretended to make us walk in the shadow of our disgrace, was jubilant about the whole affair. It was a great comfort to discover that Mr. Dow, always in sympathy with our need to explode and go upon occasions completely off the rails, was inclined to make light of our disgrace.

His presence among us produced a more tranquil climate than any Maple Street had known before. His effect upon the growing boys was quite amazing — anarchy no longer was the order of the day. Philip, more mature, did not throw water in Miss Rogers's face and hardly ever commanded her to shut up. He was in short a reformed young man. Mealtimes were a pleasure to us all. As for Miss Rogers, dear Auntie Delight, she seemed to be made anew, rejuvenated. She would descend the stairs every evening, floating like a Chopin nocturne in those gray diaphanous costumes that she loved so much. At table she habitually attempted to carry our delightful guest off and away into regions of intellectual conversation far above our heads. To this display of cloudy culture and scintillating intellect we listened fascinated, amazed that she was not in the least aware that incipient laughter trembled just below the surface of the conversation.

On the surface Mr. Dow's response was courteous, replying attentively to all she said to him; but we knew that underneath he shared our riotous recognition that she was making a perfect sketch of herself. It was hard on Grace and me, who would have liked to have saved her from her own absurdities, to choose between wanting to protect her and leading her on to furnish us with more and better entertainment.

In the evenings after supper she liked to corner him in the library for long conversations; the problem of how to manage our education was the foremost topic. She pleaded for his advice — she needed his help — she *depended* upon him. The atmosphere was charged with intimations that something romantic and sentimental was going on. Through the grapevine (that intimate network that ran from Mr. Dow to the boys to us) we learned that Miss Rogers had confided her concern for the gossip occasioned by her living unchaperoned in the house with him. She felt exposed to the censure of Springfield society. Did Mr. Dow not agree that our aunt and uncle were to blame for placing them in such a compromising position?

He assured her that it was not necessary for a lady of her refinement to have any fears for her reputation.

She knew of course that his attachment to Cousin Rebecca was the real reason for his living at Maple Street and that the decision made soon after they had installed him with us, to send her to Europe, was the latest attempt to break it up.

How well we realized later as we watched Miss Rogers so pathetically attempting to captivate Mr. Dow that what held us treading that precarious tightrope, stretched between humor on the one hand and sympathy on the other, over which our affection for her had taught us to walk with such remarkable skill, was that each of us knew exactly what was passing in the other's mind and that the slightest deviation of thought or sympathy on the part of either of us would have sent that delicate apparatus falling to the ground.

When Mr. Dow's winter at Maple Street came to an end, Miss Rogers found that she was completely unable to meet the demands of our education and by the next winter it had been decided that we were to go to the MacDuffie School, which our sister Rebecca was attending. This was a day and boarding school for girls. The boarders were all older and captivated our attention because they were already young ladies who seemed to be in the possession of mysterious charms, fascinating and enviable. Their laughter was full of secrets — their conversation was suggestive of knowledge to which we had not yet been initiated. Two of these, Helen Foster and Isabel Kimball, were the handsomest and most exciting of the lot. The first we called the queen and the second the princess and to pass either one caused our pulses to quicken and our knees to tremble. Had they noticed us? Would they stop and speak? Someday when we had been allowed to lengthen our skirts and turn our miserable pigtails into pompadours, we might perhaps be like these wonderful beings. As other young girls searched their mirrors for hints of future fascinations, we looked into each other's face. We spent so many hours inventing new characters and personalities for ourselves, plunging into the unexplored possibilities of a dozen glamorous roles.

Sometimes when sweet occurrences — an oriole concealed among the apple blossoms, a whiff of sudden perfume, the play of light and shade upon the grass — would send us rushing off, childhood at our heels, and in our heart a mutual knowledge of change in our response, we were, before we reached our destination, overtaken by some immense unfathomed need. Was it hunger? Was it yearning? What was its meaning? Discontent, impatient, no longer satisfied with childhood, we desperately wished for something, unimaginably beautiful and strange.

Twenty-three

$\mathcal{T}$IME AS IT ROLLED along turned up various events. When Mr. Dow's winter at Maple Street came to an end he simply vanished from the scene, but there were rumors that in spite of Aunt Anna and Uncle Jim, Cousin Rebecca was meeting him in secret. Miss Rogers hinted that they were secretly engaged. Visits to Goshen were not the same without him. But what with Auntie Canfield's gossip and our cousin's lovesick behavior he was not entirely absent from the scene. Our sister Rebecca was contributing more than her share of romance. She had fallen desperately in love with a young man by the name of Brewer Corcoran. She made no effort to conceal her feelings, and her most eloquent means of displaying them were her performances at the piano. Sometimes in the midst of a Beethoven sonata or a Chopin prelude, the notes growing louder and more dramatic as she worked up to a great crescendo, the ordered progression of chords would turn into a crashing of discordant sounds as though all the keys of the piano had been struck at once. And there she'd sit, her arms across the keyboard, her head upon her arms. Presently she'd rise and rush out of doors stretching out her hands as though imploring help from heaven. Rebecca was the only member of our wild and lawless family whose behavior had been on the whole quite mannerly. The boys teased her unmercifully. Philip, who was in possession of a poem she had written under the necessity no doubt of unburdening her surcharged heart, used frequently to quote his favorite line, "Only, only on my music's breast . . ." We felt the cruelty of this and did not join in. She maintained her position among us with characteristic dignity: "I do not belong to this family," she would say, "you are all cruel. You don't understand anything." She shouldn't have included us; we didn't often tease Rebecca.

There were other moments when her tempestuous affair brought happier vicissitudes, giving us an opportunity to see how love could change its aspect and its mood.

There were changes meanwhile in the boys. Philip had passed his examination for college with high marks and was entered at Harvard for the fall. In spite of the indignities that she had suffered at his hands in the past, Miss Rogers sang his praises — he had such a brilliant mind, the most intelligent member of the family — and she stood behind him, always taking his part against any criticism from the relatives. We were still in awe of him and expected at any moment to see him stiffen his fingers and come at us with the claw, hissing the terrible word, "CHOLERA." Indeed, he had not entirely relinquished his boyhood deviltry.

James, not far behind him in his studies, confidently relying on his "smile and address," was turning under our very eyes into a young man of poise and self-assurance to whom social accomplishments came as easily as breathing. He was neither conceited nor arrogant but took his handsome face and popularity completely for granted, and when Miss Rogers complained that his good looks should have been bestowed upon the girls, he blithely answered that they were quite as important to him as to his less fortunate sisters. He tended them carefully, taking great pains with the brushing of his hair, the tying of his neckties and the shining of his shoes. He had a number of girls and had chosen no single one, being sure of his conquest of them all. He preserved within himself a sensitive awareness; at the center of his being there was a gravity, a thoughtfulness about him quite in contrast to the blithe and easy manner so conspicuously displayed on the surface. He had taken at this time to writing poetry, which hinted at this subtle undercurrent. Philip was declaiming passages from Homer, Rebecca was pouring her heart out at the piano, and we, in the midst of romance, poetry, and scholarship, were caught up in the turbulent flux of awakening emotions.

Twenty-four

THIS PROPERTY TO BE SOLD

CONFRONTING US as we returned from school we saw this very large ugly sign disfiguring the lawn, putting a blight on it. We contemplated it, reading and rereading the words, each of which struck like a blow at our heart. Incapable of believing our eyes, dazed and astonished, we went into the house. Miss Rogers met us and took us into her arms. No one said a word. After some moments we exclaimed indignantly, "Who put it there, Miss Rogers?"

Feeling no longer the necessity of keeping silent, she loosed the torrent of her sorrow and her sarcasm. "Who do you think?"

"But what are we to do? Where are we to go?"

"Plans," she said. "Your aunt organizes well. Her generalship can always be relied upon. Plans," she repeated, curling her lip and placing that look of martyred resignation on her face.

The enormity of her own sad plight swept over us. Where would *she* go? What was *she* going to do when there were no Millers left on Maple Street? The weight of our feeling for her that we had carried so long, this curious mixture of detachment, sympathy and love emptied now of ridicule and humor, lay more heavily upon us than ever before; only love and pity remained.

The sign did not stay long on the front lawn. We learned in a few weeks that the house had been sold to a lady by the name of Mrs. Abby. She had a great deal of money and drove around the town with as much style as Aunt Anna. She would, so Uncle Jim declared, bring the place back to its old standards. The stable would no longer be empty, there would be horses in it, and a coachman, presumably, would live in what we had made our favorite clubroom. Everything would be swept and garnished and the bankings and the gardens would have better hands than those of Patrick Sullivan to care for them. This pleased our uncle greatly, and it was assumed that we also would feel happy to hear what wonders were presently to be worked on the dear familiar place.

Each day new developments were divulged. James would go to Geneva, Switzerland; he would start off in the late summer and be gone a year; Philip would return to Harvard; Rebecca was going to New York where the proper boarding-house had been found for her, and she would study music under a well-known teacher who had heard her play one summer in New London and pronounced her talents great. And as for us — we were to go to boarding school. We thought of the MacDuffie boarders and this helped to ease the pain of leaving home. We were not children any longer, we were young ladies. Already our skirts had been lengthened; they almost reached our ankles. And though our hair was not put up, it was tied in a knot behind with a ribbon, giving us quite the aspect of grown-up characters. We looked at each other, not with entire disapproval of what we saw. We must do our best to give up childish things — we resolved to stop our showing off forever.

In the midst of so many distressing changes we began to get ready for going to boarding school. We started to pack our trunk, for girls at boarding school must arrive with certain tokens of their status as young ladies. And we must find as many things to decorate our room as possible. Pictures of Gibson girls were favored in particular; we chose the loveliest of these beauties, trying to believe that soon we would resemble the glamorous young women with their athletic figures, the proud carriage, the hair blown back from their beautiful, perfectly stunning faces. Gibson girls and going to boarding school somehow became almost synonymous. Packing the trunk, laying up these hoarded treasures, assisted us in lessening the pain of our departure.

But we could not forget Miss Rogers, whose woeful countenance combined with her shafts of sarcasm constantly reminded us of her plight and clouded our hopes for the future and the great experiment of growing up.

There was much to be done. Mrs. Abby was anxious to move in as soon as possible. The house had to be dismantled, our belongings carefully sorted out from those that were to go to Chestnut Street, our things to be put in storage pending the day when we would all be educated and could then live together again in a home of our own. "Your aunt is a prize maker of plans. She ties her knots with precision," Miss Rogers frequently remarked.

It was really surprising to discover how thoroughly Aunt Anna had laid plans for all of us, and this in spite of the fact that she was in the midst of positively stupendous preparations for the great wedding that was to take place at Goshen in July. During the summer the boys would have a home in Springfield, boarding with the mother of a friend. Philip would find a job in the summer vacation. James would sail for Europe in the autumn and on his return from Europe the following year would continue boarding in the same household with his brother pending his going on to Harvard. Rebecca would, after the wedding, go with us to Quogue, Long Island, where a dear friend of our Aunt Anna's had a large, old-fashioned house and had agreed to take the three of us in until the opening of our boarding school, at which time Rebecca's life in New York was to begin. Meanwhile as soon as the wedding was over, Aunt Anna herself would sail for Europe for what she aptly called a much needed rest.

The only person left to shift for herself was poor Miss Rogers. And what *was* Miss Rogers going to do? She enjoyed keeping us in the dark. "The Lord will provide," was her manner of avoiding a definite answer, generally accompanied by the singing of a most melancholy hymn:

> *The foxes found rest*
> *And the birds their nest*
> *In the shade of the forest tree;*
> *But thy couch was the sod*
> *Oh thou Son of God*
> *In the desert of Galilee.*

She went about followed by Patrick Sullivan who, to console himself in the midst of the general upheaval, was enjoying a state of chronic intoxication. It was a sad thing, indeed, to look on while the beloved old home was little by little dismantled. There was the Dying Gladiator going into a barrel with the bronze Mercury, and there was the little marble girl wrapped round with excelsior being placed with Patrick's assistance in another barrel — most of the pictures were taken from the wall and now lay on the floor with their faces down; a wonder it was that Patrick did not step into them all. "And what shall I be doing now, Miss Ratchers?" he kept inquiring. She directed and he staggered about attempting to follow her directions, while to keep ourselves from succumbing to the general depression we'd run out to visit our favorite places on the bankings or the lawn.

It was May. The fruit trees were in blossom and the violets in bloom on the bankings and the weather so lovely that it seemed as we ran or stopped or lingered that we were being presented with all the accumulated memories folded and wrapped round in familiar smells and sounds and happy moments spent right here or there or in some other well-known spot where we had sniffed and looked and listened. This mysterious flow of life, of memory, we shared at this time with great intensity, for we knew that there would be no more saying to ourselves, "We'll be coming back in August," or "In another fortnight we will be home, we will see Miss Rogers." This time it would be good-bye for always.

And Miss Rogers, where would she be going? We questioned — we persisted — little by little we got it out of her. After continued urging she finally divulged the fact that she had another brother of whom we had never heard.

"I have *my* plans," she told us proudly, "I am going to my brother Will."

The existence of a second brother of whom she had never spoken presented us with as great a mystery as the disappearance of Manley. When we questioned her further she said that Will needed her. He needed a home. She wanted to be needed. That was her necessity.

And what did he do? Where did he live?

He lived, she told us, in New York. He was connected with the Customs House. She found it difficult to explain about the Customs House, and exactly what his duties were, but we gathered that they were important and had to do with travelers returning home from Europe. Nothing she said led us to imagine that her brother was as much addicted to the bottle as her favorite Patrick Sullivan, who during those melancholy days was so forlornly following her around. As the time for our parting grew nearer, she managed to make this home that she would share with Will have considerable style. It seemed he lived in an apartment that was full of fine old family possessions. And it was her intention to add to all this elegance and refinement by her presence in their midst.

She was to leave for New York the day after we departed for New London and we were cordially invited to visit her when and if we ever came to New York. We derived some comfort from knowing that there actually was a place waiting for her, though it was easy to see that she was not greatly sustained by sharing the same knowledge.

For consolation she resorted to her Bible and her prayer book, from which she quoted liberally, all this producing in her an aloofness, an unaccustomed holding back of any expression of love and tenderness or the profound sorrow that she felt at parting from us.

On the day of our departure there was no breaking down, no giving in to weakness. She did not accompany us to the station but stood at the doorway to bid us good-bye, giving us each a somewhat undemonstrative kiss, saying that she hoped our Aunt Anna would be satisfied with the wardrobe she had provided us. It was, to put it mildly, excruciating.

Twenty-five

$\mathcal{I}$T WAS THE MORNING of the wedding; would this fog that shrouded the meadows in a cloud and hid the sea from view blow off and clear away, or would it persist, growing thicker and maybe later turn into rain?

There were gleams of light inside the clouds penetrating the mist and fog; there were tents upon the lawn and strange waiters hurrying here and there, taking a squint at the sky as though uncertain; there was a glimpse of the blue sky and of the sea.

Softly, so softly, the fog rolled back. Hyacinth pink, hyacinth blue; and beneath the lifting curtain — the sea serenely calm and shining. The *Fidget* was anchored off the dock, so appropriately in the picture. Gulls rose. The birds were singing in the meadows. A perfect Goshen day.

Our spirits lifted as the weather cleared. The importance of the ceremony about to be enacted and all the celebrations that were being prepared filled us full not only of excitement but of a certain gravity, sharing as we did the human conflict that had preceded this great event.

The house was full of visitors. At the farmhouse were the boys and Mr. Dow. In less than an hour Mr. Dow would be our Cousin Louis.

It was time to prepare ourselves. We helped one another to get into our beautiful new dresses which Aunt Anna had had made for us in New York. They were white with hand embroidery, very long, almost reaching our ankles, with a pink sash for Grace and a blue one for me.

The moment had arrived. All the guests had gathered on the pavilion, at the farther end of which great banks of ferns and white roses formed a bower which awaited the members of the wedding party. The guests were arrayed in lovely summer costumes — everyone expectant, chatting, whispering, laughing. The well-known figure of our minister, Mr. Cookson, entered the rose-decked bower, and then apparently from nowhere there was Mr. Dow beside him. The chatting ceased; a string orchestra hidden behind banked greenery and palms struck up the wedding march, so deliciously disturbing in the fresh flower-scented air; Uncle Jim, very serious, appeared with Cousin Rebecca on his arm. She looked beautiful in her white satin dress, with a lace veil and a long impressive train; she was carrying a bouquet of sweet peas; Cousin Anna, her maid of honor, and all the bridesmaids carried similar bouquets and these subtly matched the exquisite and vari-hued colors of their dresses giving just the right midsummer note to the airy procession as it passed by. The ushers walked behind with white rosebuds in their buttonholes.

The music stopped. The members of the wedding party distributed themselves in the flowery bower and Cousin Rebecca and Mr. Dow stood in front of the white-robed Mr.

Cookson who loomed ministerially in front of them, prayer book in hand. The ceremony began. Conscious of our dresses, which induced in us a sense of growing into a new maturity, we stood there together listening. The beauty and solemnity of the wedding service almost overwhelmed us. We experienced a moment of perfect and complete communion. A thought that we had never had before struck us suddenly: we ourselves could *never* marry — impossible! We considered the decision, weighing it carefully. We who had always and would always share the same feelings and had bestowed our loves and hates, our likes and dislikes, upon everyone with equal fervor —

". . . *For better, for worse, for richer, for poorer, in sickness and in health* . . ."

— for one of us to choose someone to marry without the other twin determining to marry him too was out of the question. Without a spoken word between us, we realized that we had not until this moment understood the implications in the bond that made us one. Mr. Dow slipped the ring on Cousin Rebecca's finger.

Twenty-six

$\mathcal{I}$T WAS ALL OVER, they were married. The orchestra started playing a second wedding march, gayer than the first. Conversation and laughter began and we too were mixing with the crowd. Everyone was getting in line to congratulate the bride and groom. The boys and Rebecca and the two of us were on our way to kiss Cousin Rebecca and our new cousin, Mr. Dow. Such a rush and bustle of activities, the crowd mingling and intermingling. Small tables were set up on the pavilion and on the lawn, and a long table for the bridal party was being arranged in the bower where the ceremony took place. We enjoyed the moment and the scene intensely, feeling very close to each other and a little set apart — as always. Philip beckoned us. He had found a table for all of us. The wedding breakfast was delightful, there was champagne and there were boxes of wedding cake tied with white ribbon for everyone. This was the most splendid spectacle that we had ever seen at Goshen. Sipping our champagne, a little bemused, we left the conversation mostly to Rebecca and the boys, sharing our sense of being in the midst of something quite extraordinary.

When the breakfast was over and the boys and Rebecca had wandered away, we wondered where to go and what we had better do with ourselves. Struck by the same idea, we ran down into the meadow where the grass was cut and the hay cocked in many fragrant piles. Down there in the stubble grass there would be plenty of clover and, if we looked carefully, we would be able to find some with four leaves and these we would pick and bring up to the bride to place in her shoe when she went off. The birds were singing, blending their notes with the music of the orchestra behind us. This was a place that made us happy. Here we had experienced so much joy. It might be we had left childhood behind us, but here we would always feel that we were children. We lingered, we searched, we stood erect and looked about us, taking in the entrancing scene — the laughter and the voices and the music. We were determined to search until we found what we were looking for. What a blue perfect day. There was quite a breeze and there were whitecaps on the water and the gulls were dipping in the sea. We would be content to stay until the great show was over, but time was passing by and we must stop and count our four-leaf clovers. Finally discovering that we had six between us, we rushed back to the pavilion, where we found Cousin Rebecca and offered them to her to put in her shoes when she went off with Mr. Dow. She was delighted with our gift. We wished her good luck and happiness for ever and our gesture and those moments in the meadow seemed to us the happiest part of that auspicious day.

There was a big letdown after the wedding. Aunt Anna had packed and gone to Europe; the bride and groom had disappeared, no one knew just where; Uncle Jim and Cousin Anna and some visitors still remained. The weather, the fine Goshen weather continued. We hoarded the days because we knew that we would soon be leaving for Quogue. Every night we crossed off a day on the calendar — only six more days now, only five, we would tell each other.

On the last day before departure our reluctance to leave took shape in a mood of reminiscence and regret. As Grace could not go in the water, I decided to remain with her while the others bathed. We thought about our last days at Maple Street; it was impossible to think we would not return again. Who would enjoy the bankings? Imagine Mrs. Abby devouring the grapes and Seckel pears. Who would rake up the leaves and jump into the bonfires and what, we wondered, had become of Patrick Sullivan?

We heard them calling, crying out how wonderful the water was, how refreshing. There were shouts and calls and splashes. We wished that we were bathing with them, but we lay as we had done so many times before, enjoying the heat of the sand as it struck at us and warmed us through and through, doing what we used to do when we were children, picking out the tiny grains of colored sand and showing them to one another. It was a game no longer, only an old habit lazily indulged in.

Crystal waves were breaking with a sound of tinkling glass and shattered sunlight. They drew back, crunching the pebbles with a deeper pebbly murmur. They broke and retreated — when would we hear the lovely sound again?

"Here's a sapphire, Mary, and here's a ruby."

"Here's a topaz."

Uncle Jim came out of his bathhouse and emptied a pail of salt water over the railing. "What," he said, "aren't the twins bathing?"

"Not today," we answered and we thought that tomorrow we would be at Quogue. And we wondered how we would like it there. Two weeks from today would be our birthday. We would be fourteen.

"Can you remember, Grace, how we used to rip off our shoes and stockings and wade among the rocks looking for little crabs? We'll not be doing that again."

Quogue was near Montauk. Maybe we would see the light in the New London lighthouse. Small, transparent shell-like creatures jumped from the sand and hit our faces. The air wavered before our eyes like water on a sheet of glass. The heat struck through our bodies, warming us. Only a month and three weeks more and we would be at boarding school. Summer swam and swarmed around us. The smell of sand, the smell of the salt sea, the music of the water. And it seemed sad to think that childhood was behind us.

Twenty-seven

Quogue was different from Goshen. For a while we were forlorn indeed, but we were conscious of feeling a bit excited too, for in both our minds was the knowledge that from now on everything was bound to be different and life, we recognized, could not but be interesting wherever we might be.

The house in which we found ourselves reminded us of Maple Street. It was plain enough that sufficient funds to keep it up to former standards were lacking. The furniture needed re-upholstering; the rugs were worn and shabby. As for the walls, what they lacked in fresh paint or newly designed wallpapers, they more than made up for in family portraits. Ancestors looked down at us from every room; their assumption of arrogance and importance gave us a sense of ancestry that accorded little with our kindly and unassuming hostesses.

Mrs. Hodge was as unlike her old schoolmate, our Aunt Anna, as it was possible for anyone to be. She did not reprimand us, or inspect our wardrobes, and was inclined to take our grown-up role more for granted than that of children needing constant supervision. She was much more concerned about Rebecca than about us, as she had no friends of her own age with whom to associate, and when she received an invitation to visit a school friend who lived in Lawrence, a place at no great distance, Mrs. Hodge willingly allowed her to accept. We were sad to see her go; her departure bereft us of the last shred of our past existence.

Mrs. Hodge had an unmarried daughter approaching thirty; she was plain but exceedingly kind; she played croquet with us and allowed us to beat her at anagrams every evening. Then there was also Miss Madeleine Stone, a niece of Mrs. Hodge's. She was beautiful; she had honey-colored hair and a pale complexion under which pulsed a faint suggestion of color like a blush about to rise and suffuse her face. Her voice was low and thrilling; we loved to be in the same room with her. She created a climate in which we practiced good manners and the fascinating arts of becoming young ladies.

We stood on a threshold on one side of which lay an unknown future and on the other side all our familiar memories. To go forward was to conjure with infinite possibilities; to go back was to retreat into childhood, which was so completely our own that we clung to it as to a personality from which we were loath to part.

The days went by. We were much out of doors. Here there was no beach, no open glimpse of sea; we were on an inlet, there were marshes, rushes and mosquitoes and we were allowed to go down to a landing where there was a flat-bottom boat and oars and we were in the habit of rowing every day. This became the pleasantest thing about our visit — getting into our bathing suits and rowing or floating about at our own discretion. We discovered a fascinating game that we played when we were rowing, venturing forth on ever longer journeys in search of buoys which we enjoyed picking up and displacing. We did not exactly know what buoys were and we found it exciting to displace them, lending a little spice to days that seemed very slow and uneventful.

The sixth of August was our birthday. We had a cake and candles and some presents but it was a little sad; we received a letter from Miss Rogers, restrained and undemonstrative, in which she said more about Aunt Anna than about herself. Her brother was well and glad to have her with him. There was much to do to put their new home in order. She understood our aunt had taken a house in New York for the coming winter and hoped that she would see us then.

Where would we be next winter? Would we stay with Aunt Anna in New York? Probably we would. That must be among her plans. Then we would see Miss Rogers, and Rebecca would be studying music; James would be in Europe. Thinking of all these things and going out in the boat we had at our disposal, the days passed by. There was a fog most every morning, and then the fog blew off and we would float between the hazy sky and the still water, dreaming a good deal, thinking of yesterday and of tomorrow — making plans, imagining.

One day there was no fog; the air was clarion clear and the sky was blue and cloudless with a brisk breeze blowing and just a touch of autumn in the weather — enough to set the heart in motion toward the future. We started off dressed in our bathing suits as usual, feeling extraordinarily exultant. Embarking on our inland waters that flowed so swiftly toward the sea we made all manner of plans about our future.

We rowed a bit, we drifted, we found a buoy and dragged it up and let it go, and when the sun grew warmer we slipped over the side of the boat and began, as had been our custom, hanging onto the gunwale with one hand and swimming with the other, to enjoy this cool fresh summer water. Laughing and shouting we let go the gunwale; we swam around the boat, and then a little puff of wind — the boat was carried off and away and headed for the outlet and the sea. Suddenly filled with panic we did our best to overtake it, swimming as swiftly as was possible; but this we saw was hopeless, a futile thing to do — to waste strength necessary to swim ashore. We were lost and terrified — Grace's strength already spent. Was she clinging to me? No, she was not, she was still beside me in the water, swimming still. What was it she was saying? Clearly I heard her voice; as though I myself were speaking the words, she said, "My darling Mary, how I love you . . ."

Then there was silence and I saw she was not there beside me. Where was she? Where was I?

I called to her, "Float, Grace, get over on your back, float, keep on floating."

And where was I? What was I doing? Where was I going?

"Float, Grace," I called, and with all the strength that still remained I swam, I kept on swimming toward the shore and always calling, "Float, Grace, keep floating." And even when I'd reached the bank and was running toward the nearest house I kept shouting but it was not my voice I heard.

The voice was hers.

"My darling Mary, how I love you."

An Afterword

$\mathcal{T}$HE DESIRE and pursuit of the whole is what is called love."

The last words Grace spoke to me were an affirmation of the fact that our childhood, which was so rudely terminated on that August afternoon, had been complete and round — a perfect whole.

That business in which we are all perpetually engaged — the making of an individual soul — is an enterprise of memory. In our case it was a joint and not a single venture.

I am an old woman now and full of many memories, but those which I have here evoked have for me still the strange and wonderful completeness of having lived another's life that was at the same time my own.

Mary and Grace Miller

BY JAMES MILLER

*R*EADERS OF *UNDER GEMINI* will of course recognize the strength of the love Mary felt for her sister Grace, but I think only those who knew Mary well can be aware of the importance to her of the niche that Grace continued to occupy in her mind for the seventy-eight years Mary lived after her sister's death. My wife Nancy and I saw much of her during the last thirty of those years, and often one of us would remark, after spending a dinner or an evening with her which included some reminiscing by her about Grace, how very rare it was to have such a visit without some mention of Grace managing to pop up in the conversation.

Indeed, there is no question that Mary's favorite "comfortable" subject of conversation, the one she'd wrap around her like a cozy shawl when the talk on weightier matters began to pale, was Grace and the joys of "the bond that made us one." When *Under Gemini* was published in 1966 and Nancy and I read it for the first time, many of its phrases — "the wondrous apparatus of our twinship," "the words that issue from her tongue are mine," "a creature whose response to everything I experienced appeared to be identical and simultaneous with my own" — were already familiar to us from these many talks. She would talk about these things with anyone who would listen. "If you ever mentioned the name Grace in Mary's presence," says Tobias Schneebaum, the twenty-year neighbor and "Incomparable Friend" to whom she dedicated *Under Gemini,* "you knew you were starting at least a half-hour's conversation."

Indeed, so important to her was the memory of Grace that in the mid 60's, more than half a century after Grace's death, when Mary's publisher asked her to prepare an autobiographical sketch, she began it with these words: "I was born only five minutes, so the legend goes, after my sister. This participation in identical twinship is the most valuable experience of my life. It is the source of whatever insight into human nature or response to the beauties and mysteries of the natural world I may possess." Aside from this sketch, the only other attempts she made at autobiographical writing were her first novel, *In The Days of Thy Youth,* and *Under Gemini* — and in both of these Grace was the major presence beside herself, and both books ended at the moment of Grace's death.

In all of Nancy's and my conversations with Mary about Grace, she never, ever talked about the tragic side of the story — the years after Grace when she had to learn to face the world alone. Her talk was always limited to the decade (1887–1897) described in *Under Gemini,* which she regarded as the happy years — i.e., the ones in which, despite the many problems the twins encountered, she and Grace had each other. The only explicit reference I am aware of that she ever made to the dark years was in the autobiographical sketch referred to above: "In my fourteenth year my twin sister was drowned. After this there seems to be a blotting out of life — everything becomes dim, unreal, artificial . . ." She doesn't say how long the blotted-out period lasted, and aside from mentioning that she finished boarding school and traveled in Europe for an unspecified period of time, she tells nothing about her specific activities during these years.

However, it seems probable to Nancy and me that at some time during this period Grace's death took its toll on her in the form of an emotional collapse. Once, when we were talking with her about the beauty of the New England countryside, she remarked that when she'd been very young she'd found the peacefulness of the Berkshire Hills to have a remarkably therapeutic effect on her at a time when she was "getting over a bad experience" (in what we gathered was a sanatarium not far from Springfield). This and a similar remark she made to Tobias are the only facts we have to back our belief. But given the nature of Mary's bond with Grace, and the horror of the way it was finally broken (along with the guilt that one could expect to flow from her own role in the breaking of it) — and the fact that she was only fourteen at the time it happened — such a reaction would certainly not have been surprising.

When Mary died in 1975 and Nancy and I went to her apartment to gather her effects, one of the first things we came across was a final indication of the steadfastness of her devotion to Grace. In the center pigeon hole of her desk, directly in front of her as she wrote, was a letter-sized envelope containing three objects. One was a lock of Grace's hair. Another was the original copy of the Western Union Telegraph Company form sent from New London Aug. 12, 1897, in which her guardian, Uncle Jim, informed his family of

Grace's drowning. And the third was a sixteen-line poem in Mary's handwriting, presumably written seventy-eight years earlier, that was titled "Grace" and whose last eight lines were:

> *How happy you must be, my Grace,*
> *With an angel on each side*
> *And God's own tender loving face*
> *So near you now to guide*
>
> *But Grace should I not then be proud*
> *And neither sigh nor weep*
> *For some day I will be allowed*
> *To come to you and sleep.*

> — JAMES MILLER, *Nephew of Mary Britton Miller*
> Crugers, New York
> December 24, 1998

A NOTE ON THE AUTHOR

ISABEL BOLTON was the pen name of Mary Britton Miller. She wrote poetry and children's verse under the name Miller until, in her sixties, she began writing serious novels under the pseudonym of Isabel Bolton. Three of her novels, *Do I Wake or Sleep, The Christmas Tree,* and *Many Mansions,* have been collected in the omnibus, *New York Mosaic.* She lived from 1883 to 1975.

A NOTE ON THE BOOK

THE TEXT for this book was composed by Steerforth Press using a digital version of Legacy, a typeface designed by Ronald Arnholm and first issued by the International Typeface Corporation in 1993. Legacy is a revival of Nicolas Jensen's types as seen in the 1470 Eusebius. Jensen's beautiful types have been models for several typefaces since they were cut in the fifteenth century: this hand-drawn Jensen revival maintains much of the beauty and character of the original. All Steerforth books are printed on acid free papers, and this book was bound by BookCrafters of Chelsea, Michigan.